£5
18110

09905023

GW00362804

SU
COUN

CHARLIE CROKER

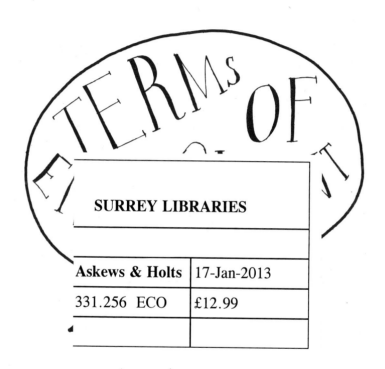

TERMS OF

THE SECRET LINGO
OF THE WORKPLACE

Published by Random House Books 2012

2 4 6 8 10 9 7 5 3 1

First published in Great Britain in 2012 by Random House Books
Random House, 20 Vauxhall Bridge Road, London SW1V 2SA

www.randomhouse.co.uk

Addresses for companies within The Random House Group
Limited can be found at: www.randomhouse.co.uk/offices.htm

The Random House Group Limited Reg. No. 954009

A CIP catalogue record for this book
is available from the British Library

ISBN 9781847946843

The Random House Group Limited supports The Forest
Stewardship Council (FSC®), the leading international forest
certification organisation. Our books carrying the FSC label are
printed on FSC® certified paper. FSC is the only forest certification
scheme endorsed by the leading environmental organisations,
including Greenpeace. Our paper procurement policy can be
found at www.randomhouse.co.uk/environment

Mixed Sources
Product group from well-managed
forests and other controlled sources
www.fsc.org Cert no. TT-COC-2139
© 1996 Forest Stewardship Council
FSC

Produced by The Curved House
Printed and bound in Great Britain by CPI Group (UK) Ltd, Croydon, CR0 4YY

Contents

Introduction

Does your job involve you **spinning someone's drum**? Or **hosing a Doris**? Or possibly **swinging for the fences**? If so you're a policeman ('spinning a drum' meaning searching a property), or a photographer (to 'hose a Doris' is to take multiple shots of a female celebrity) or a share trader (when you 'swing for the fences' you attempt a hugely ambitious trade, the analogy being taken from baseball). Every trade and profession has its own slang, the terms and lingo that only those involved in it will understand. Peeping behind the linguistic curtains to examine that slang is a fascinating endeavour. Not only does it reveal truths about the people engaged in various lines of work, it also teaches us a lot about our use of language itself.

Ego-pricing, if you're an estate agent, refers to a client's insistence on an unrealistically high valuation for their property. **Sky hooks** are mythical devices referred to by architects: a bad building, they say, will need them to stand up. Plumbers, meanwhile, have their **rabbit ears** (pipe-cutters), and bricklayers their **herringbones** (diagonal patterns in their bricks). However you earn your living, it seems, there's a private language used only by you and your colleagues. Sometimes this will be a witty piece of shorthand for something the outside world already knows about. Faking worthless furniture to make it look antique, for instance, is known to those in the business as the **carcass trade**. Sometimes, however, the slang is for something that the rest of us had no idea about in the first place. Auctioneers, for example, will sometimes **take a bid off the wall** – pretend to have seen an entirely fictitious bidder purely to drive up the price.

Some words can mean different things to different trades. American vaudeville performers understood a **fish** to be a bad act. Professional gamblers, on the other hand, use the term for the loser at a table. The implication in both cases is similar – a bad act stinks like a fish, while the gambler's poor luck might rub off as easily as a fishy smell. For criminals, on the other hand, there's an entirely different connotation: a **fish** is a first-time prisoner (as in 'out of water'). And if you're a roadie, **feeding the fish** means throwing used plectrums to the crowd at the end of a gig. A **Fishhead**, in contrast, is a member of the Navy.

At least it is if you're a member of the Army, who invented the derogatory term for their seafaring colleagues.

Indeed making yourself feel superior to others in your own line of work is a crucial function of workplace slang. Gardening firms who pride themselves on doing a thorough (if expensive) job refer to less scrupulous firms by the term **hoe, mow, blow and go**. More often, however, the aim is to put distance between you and those outside your trade. 'Backslang', started by nineteenth-century retailers and now most commonly associated with butchers, is a classic example of this. One South London butcher, seeing an unwelcome customer approaching, would say to his colleague '**tuck the dillo woc a tib of dillo woc**' — 'cut the old cow a bit of old cow'.

Occasionally the meaning is hidden for kinder reasons: some doctors write **DIFFC** on a patient's notes to conceal their certainty that there's nothing actually wrong with them, and that they just 'Dropped In For a Friendly Chat'.

Looking at how slang has changed over time is an intriguing way of seeing how the world of work itself has changed. Eighteenth-century criminals talked of the **morning sneak**, a way of burgling a house by creeping in while the domestic servant was cleaning the front doorstep. Hard to achieve that now – but other lingo has come along to take its place. Unscrupulous share traders can commit the crime of **painting the tape** – buying quantities of a stock with collaborators so that other investors see the movement on the electronic ticker tape and buy into it, thereby inflating its price.

Much of the time, of course, slang is there simply for the sake of simplicity, so members of the profession can avoid repeating the same cumbersome wording over and over again. Software engineers, for instance, would find it tedious to constantly refer to 'a sacrificial file, employed purely to observe the behaviour of a computer virus, a task it completes by carrying a sample of that virus, isolated to enable it to be monitored'. Instead they refer to a **goat file**. Terms can also be coined to show black humour, thereby allowing an outlet for cynicism about your job that might otherwise prove corrosive. Middle managers, for instance, are sometimes referred to by colleagues on other levels of the management tree as the **blobocracy**. Airline staff refer to passengers as **SLF** (Self-Loading Freight).

Whatever the reason for the workplace wordplay, every job has its own special lingo. So let's open the factory doors, peer over the office partitions and sneak around the shopfloors with our ears open and our pens at the ready. It's time to learn some terms of employment ...

ACKNOWLEDGEMENTS

Many thanks to the countless people who shed linguistic light on their jobs and professions. From the world of the stage special mention should go to actors Toby Longworth and Chris Pavlo. Ex-army boys Chris Cherrington and James Charlesworth were faultless on parade with the military slang. Chris Fickling of Ibrow Media got his fingers inky for the section on printers, while the star journos with their stubby pencils were Patrick Hennessy and Chris Hope.

I'm hugely grateful too to Tim Bentinck, John Emerson and Emma Clarke for opening up the world of advertising, Steven Hitchcock and Patrick Grant for teaching me about tailoring, and Annie Murchie and David Long for revealing the mysteries of the car trade. Chefs' terms were provided by Arthur Potts Dawson, Sophie Laurimore and Oliver Macmillan of the Swan in Long Melford, Pete Brown brewed up some good beer slang, while Graeme Ferguson was my legal eagle when it came to solicitors' lingo.

Jonathan Collett, Jerry Hayes and Paul Twinn explained political slang, Lee Jackson showed his expertise in Victorian London by pointing me towards the street beggars' codes, and Kim Vousden of the St Bride Library helped locate some great printers' terms. When it came to the world of auctions Julian Roup and Colin Sheaf at Bonhams really brought the hammer down, while Martin Roffey yet again proved himself King of the Square Mile.

Rowan Powell, Kristen Harrison and the team at The Curved House have done a wonderful job of putting the pages together. And finally, thanks go as ever to Sophie Lazar, Nigel Wilcockson, Gemma Wain and Amelia Harvell at Random House, and to Special Agent Charlie Viney.

TRANSPORT

TRANSPORT

The simple task of getting you from A to B – or selling you a vehicle that will accomplish the same feat – has given rise to more slang than you could shake a sat-nav at. London cabbies talk about going **over the hump** (driving to the City via Angel rather than High Holborn), American truck drivers refer to themselves as **tanker yankers**, while airline staff call the emergency oxygen masks the **rubber jungle**. Work in any of these transport fields and you'll be finding your way around the language ...

London cabbies

They can take you from the **Gasworks** (the Houses of Parliament) to the **Pancake** (St Pancras Station), or from the **Dead Zoo** (the Natural History Museum) to the **Uproar** (the Royal Opera House). Other locations include:

American Workhouse – the Park Lane Hotel (popular with Americans)

Aztec Temple – the imposing MI6 HQ at Vauxhall

The Bone – Marylebone Station

The Gas Chamber – Euston Station taxi rank (it's underground, and also known as **The Pit**)

The Kremlin – cab shelter by Albert Bridge

The Dirty Dozen – twelve roads through Soho that get you from Regent Street to Charing Cross Road without having to go along busy Oxford Street

Fagin's Kitchen – the Stock Exchange (also known as the **Den of Thieves**)

Hole In The Wall – Wilton Road entrance to Victoria Station

Honeypot – the West End

Kangaroo Valley – Earls Court (traditionally popular with Australians)

The Loo – Waterloo Station

Magic Roundabout – Shepherd's Bush Green

Magic Circle – Piccadilly Circus and surrounding area

McLiver – Liverpool Street taxi rank (by McDonald's)

Padders – Paddington Station

PG Tips – Palace Gardens Terrace

The Pipe – The Blackwall Tunnel

The Resistance – Harley Street, because doctors opposed the formation of the NHS. (Also known as **Pill Island**)

Royal Lobster – Kings Cross Station (i.e. 'King Crustacean')

The Saveloy – the Savoy

The Tripe Shop – Broadcasting House

The Wedding Cake – The Queen Victoria Memorial outside Buckingham Palace, which has remained white since it was built in 1911

The capital's cabbies don't restrict their slang to place names. They start their careers as **butterboys** (a new cabbie – you are 'but a boy'), get their first **sherbert** ('sherbert dab' – taxi cab), and pray it won't be **kipper season** (any time of year when business is a bit slack, from when cabbies could only afford to eat kippers instead of steak). They may have to endure a **binder** (a very long wait at a rank, also known as **roasting**), and pray for a **flyer** (a lucrative fare to one of the airports). A warning – they're not happy if you **legal** them (pay the exact fare without adding a tip).

blue trees – policemen hiding while checking for speeding drivers (the speed gun they use being known as a **hairdryer** – or the officer himself as a **Kojak with a Kodak**)

bottle – £2 (i.e. 'bottle of glue')

broom – refuse an unwanted job, which cabbies technically aren't allowed to do (also known as **brushing**)

butterfly – a cabbie who only works in the summer

canaries – Yellow Badge drivers (the ones permitted to work only in London's suburbs)

Churchill – a meal (Winston Churchill gave cabbies the right to refuse a fare while eating)

copperbottom – cabbie who's been driving for a long spell

hickory – the fare meter (i.e. 'hickory dickory dock' – clock) (also **zeiger**)

Louis Vuitton – a good fare

musher – an owner driver, as opposed to a driver who rents his cab (a **journeyman**). Therefore **musher's lotion** is rain

on point – at the front of a rank, next in line to get a punter

on the cotton – used while doing the Knowledge – a route that's as straight as possible, checked by putting a piece of string on the map

putting on foul – joining a taxi rank that's already full

roader – a long journey, normally to outside the London boroughs

Male and female passengers are **cocks** and **hens** respectively, while a **single pin** is one on his or her own. People emerging from a venue at the end of a concert are said to be **on the burst**, and will form a **Mexican wave**.

The ex-head of the Royal Navy Admiral West, during his time as a minister in Gordon Brown's government, was forced to do a speedy U-turn on home office policy (due to not knowing that the official position had changed). Travelling in a taxi a short time later his cabbie, who didn't know who he was, had to turn round in the road. 'Sorry about this guv,' said the driver. 'Just got to do an **Admiral West**.'

Lorry drivers

British lorry drivers refer to a penknife as a **rope spanner**. Their Australian counterparts use **flash for cash** to denote a speed camera, and **turd herder** for a driver carrying animal freight. Meanwhile in America there's ...

barbershop – a low bridge (could take your top off)

city kitty – a city policeman (as opposed to a county mounty, a county sheriff, or a full grown, a state trooper)

deadhead – a cab pulling an empty trailer

double-nickel – 55 mph

hammer lane – the outside lane (as opposed to the inside one, which is the **granny lane**)

piggy bank – a toll booth

Railways

The 1960s was a golden age for the British railways – at least when it came to slang. Drivers would refer to **cauliflowers** (locomotives with a crest on the front) or **killers** (diesel units – you couldn't hear them coming), possibly on **kipper trips** (special services laid on for anglers) or **up the madhouse** (any train heading into London). They encountered **number snatchers** (checkers of goods wagons), **rabbits** (short distance travellers) and **razor gangs** (men sent from HQ to find economy measures).

alleluia – a call to shut the tap when boiler washing

bug dust – small coal (coal ovoids were known as **duck eggs**)

Cinderella's coach – the District Engineer's coach

fluff – porters' tips (selecting the luggage of rich passengers to carry was known as **fluffing**)

in the dirt – derailed

the Kremlin – British Railways' HQ

lollipop – a tool, used for testing sleepers, that had a long shaft with an iron ball on the end

one Labour gain – a yellow light at a colour signal

the Owl – the Paddington to Penzance night train

Prince of Wales – an engine blowing off steam

pull the monkey – drag a rubber disc through a cess drain to clean it

ride on the cushions – an engine man travelling as a passenger

sparkler – an electric train

spiv day – a rest day

thrombosis – a traffic apprentice (i.e. 'a bloody clot wandering around the system')

two crows for a banker – coded whistles exchanged between the engine and the second banking engine when ready to move

Before nationalisation, different areas of the country were served by different private companies. These soon acquired their own unofficial names:

L.M.S (London, Midland and Scottish Railway) – **Ell of a mess**

Lancashire and Yorkshire Railway – **the Languisher and Yawner**

London and North Eastern Railway – **Late and Never Early**

Manchester, Sheffield and Lincolnshire Railway – **Muck, Sludge and Lightning**

Oxford, Worcester and Wolverhampton Railway – **Old Worser and Worser**

Somerset and Dorset Railway – **Slow and Dirty**

South Eastern and Chatham Railway – **Slow, Easy and Comfortable**

On the American railroads there are **black snakes** (loaded coal trains) and **pig palaces** (livestock trains). If you **go to beans** you eat lunch. A **stinger** is a brakeman, a **bake head** is a fireman and a **foamer** denotes a railway enthusiast. In Australia the latter is a **gunzel**. Other slang from Down Under includes **bun ticket** for meal allowance, **bustitute** for a bus replacement service and **death warrant** for the form signed by a railway enthusiast, waiving the train company's liability and allowing them to travel in the van of a goods train.

Airlines

Up, up and away we go – into a world where in-flight catering is **animal control**, where passengers are **SLF** (self-loading freight) and deep vein thrombosis is known as **jet leg**. Airline staff have a whole host of terms, not just for customers but for themselves too. Stewardesses are **cart tarts**, while British Airways pilots are known to the rest of the industry as **Nigels**. Maritime patrol pilots searching an area of sea in a grid system are said to **mow the lawn**. But it's over the pond, in the American airline industry, that slang has really, ahem, taken off ...

boredom tube – a plane

George – autopilot

fish finder – TCAS screen (Traffic Collision Avoidance System), displayed in the cockpit

rabbit – runway light used to help with landings (sometimes a pilot will ask Air Traffic Control to **kill the rabbit**)

Smurf juice – blue disinfectant used in toilets (hence the toilet is known as the **blue room**)

bugle bag – sick bag (also known as a **happy sack**)

pilot pellets – peanuts

hockey pucks – mini-sandwiches served to passengers. Also the small filet mignons served in first class.

Passengers are **peeps**, **monkeys** or **pax**, unless they're children carried on parents' laps, in which case they're **lava** or **cabin missiles**. A fat passenger is a **customer of size**, while a good-looking female one is a **BOB** (babe on board). An old Pan-Am term for a male passenger with an over-zealous interest in stewardesses was **stew bum**.

One system of flying regulations was known as 'Extended Operations' or 'ETOPS' – pilots said that this stood for **Engines Turn or People Swim**.

slam dunk – a steep descent (also known as a **Baghdad approach**)

deadhead – to travel free of charge on one of your airline's flights, without working

pilot error – a pregnant stewardess

galley queen – a lazy stewardess who hides in the galley

charm farm – training school for stewards and stewardesses

ramp rats – ground handling crews

plucker – the attendant who checks passengers' tickets as they board the plane

stew zoo – apartment or hotel where stewards and stewardesses stay between flights

sky bag – carry-on luggage

Nashville Samsonite – plastic bin bag in which some passengers carry their belongings

bottle to throttle time – the period (commonly 12 hours) before a flight during which attendants are forbidden from drinking alcohol

American Airlines refer to any dead body being transported in the hold as **Jim Wilson**

The old AA flight from Austin to San Jose, used mainly by technology workers, was known as the **nerd bird**

American aerospace engineering

A complex industry, this one. You can **eat an elephant** (solve a difficult problem by splitting it into smaller tasks), **get the customer pregnant** (involve them financially and technically in your project to such an extent that they won't be able to pull out), or **screw the pooch** (lose something expensive because of negligence – from the astronaut Gus Grissom, who opened a hatch on a Mercury capsule and sank it). There might be **a camel getting its nose into the tent** (a person or firm entering a project who will eventually come to dominate it and push you out), a **group grope** (a large meeting or review), or a **hello phone** (one used to contact a top-secret programme, 'hello' being the only word said when answering it).

give an elephant an enema – start a process that will be slow at first but then become unstoppable

assholes and elbows – everybody working hard (e.g. 'When the manager comes to inspect, all I want to see in this lab is assholes and elbows')

East Armpit – any remote location for a field test

sand to suit – adapt a standard piece of equipment to your individual needs

Glyp it and ship it – finish something quickly (Glyptol is a clear substance used to hold coils in place)

IFU – engineers (i.e. 'Interchangeable Faceless Units')

jelly beans – commonplace electronic components

nine women, one month – put excessive numbers of people onto a project in the futile hope of expediting it. (Said to be how NASA would make a baby.)

show the flag – visit a customer purely to show interest/activity, rather than to achieve anything substantial

shake and bake – environmental testing, involving vibration and heat testing

wear your work gloves – stand with hands in pockets

The high-altitude aeroplane used by NASA to train their astronauts in zero-gravity conditions (by flying on a parabolic trajectory) was known as the **vomit comet**

⚓ Merchant navy ⚓

Transporting things across the oceans can give rise to slang too, as anyone in the merchant navy will tell you. Whether they're munching on a **tabnab** (any small snack) or keeping the right side of the **bully beef** (the Chief Engineer), working on the **big locker** (as the sea is known in the Australian merchant navy) is a verbal assault course.

The Brits can be **ginger beers** (engineers), also known by the first half of the phrase **oil and water** (engineers and deck officers – said not to mix with each other). The **wardroom** is the bar, a **smoke-co** is a cigarette and coffee break, while **turn to** means to work.

Australians, meanwhile, might hit **holes in the road** (a choppy sea) and end up **calling for Herb** (vomiting violently). Much better to be cruising at **100 fathoms** (sound asleep) or **conducting a deckhead survey** (lying in your bunk, the deckhead being the ceiling) on your **donkey's breakfast** (mattress – they used to be filled with straw). If you're really lucky you might find yourself **in the lee of Bum Island** (in bed with a woman). The **coffee grinder** is the ship's steering wheel, while a **cranno** is a haircut (short for cranium).

Meanwhile on the shore, Australian dock workers used to refer to **1 o'clock militants** – workers who were quiet in the morning but combative with management after returning from a liquid lunch. Such workers were said to have had a **few pots of unionism.**

Car industry

Just put some **sky in your boots?** Paid your **rent** and **got a ticket?** Or are you looking to **add a blower** to your **Henry?** If so you probably work in the car industry, and have put air in your tyres, paid your road tax and obtained an MOT, and want to attach a turbocharger to your Ford. For the rest of you – pull down your **hole in the head** (sunroof), and feel the wind in your hair as we zoom through some more car trade lingo ...

wind and skin are air conditioning and leather upholstery, while if a car lacks the former it's a **Kojak** (i.e. 'no 'air').

bidet – rear window washer

dizzy hat – distributor cap

fast glass (Australia) – electric windows

Jesus handles – interior handles (because that's what anyone holding onto them will be screaming)

roo catcher (Australia) – bull bars on front of vehicle

picnic table – a boot spoiler

rubber hankies – windscreen wipers

slush box – automatic transmission

hog leg – a gearstick that comes up from the floor (also known as a **John Holmes**, after the porn star)

tar – diesel, as used in a **clacker** – a car with a diesel engine (also **smoker**)

kiss – a minor accident that caused no damage (in Australia: **love tap**)

scamera – a speed camera

booze bus (Australia) – car used by police doing random breathalyser tests

human handbrake (Australia) – passenger who constantly complains about high speed

temporary Australian (Australia) – motorcycle rider

ape-hanger (US) – drop handlebars on a motorbike

Cars to avoid include the **Diana Ross** (one that's worth less than the outstanding finance due on it, as in Ross's song 'Upside Down'), and the **Beatle** (a badly-dented one – 'more hits than the Beatles'). A bad car is a **lemon**, a **shed** or **carbage**. One that's **leggy** has got a high mileage (in America it may have a **buck-twenty-five on the clock** – 125,000 miles), while a **rainbow warrior** is a car that's been repainted many times. Avoid **90 Day Bloom**, a particular colour known as Solid Blue (it never sells, so you'll still have the car on your forecourt in 90 days' time). A **pov spec** (short for 'poverty specification') is a basic model of a car with no added extras. Salesmen who try to disguise a poor-quality car have been known to utter the mantra **'you can't polish a turd, but you can roll it in glitter'**.

The opposite of all this in the US is a **cream puff** – a used car in excellent condition (also **out of the wrapper**)

halo car (US) – a high-end model that lends prestige to a manufacturer's other cars

crotch rocket – fast motorbike

Yank tank (Australia) – any American car

sushi sledge – any Japanese car

left hooker – a left-hand drive car

rag top – a convertible

shopping trolley – a small hatchback

weapon – a very fast car

Need to get even more specific? Here are how various brands are known around the world:

Bitsaremissing (Australia) – Mitsubishi

In America BMW is said to stand, depending on your point of view, for **Beautiful Mechanical Wonder** or **Burn My Wallet**

Eccy – a Ford Escort

Fezza – a Ferrari

Hardly Driveable (Australia) – Harley-Davidson

Landy – a Land Rover

lawyer killer (US) – a Porsche 911 Turbo

Porker – a Porsche

Pug – a Peugeot

About to buy a secondhand car? You might want to know how the salesmen talk about you first. If you're a **wallet** (easy to sell to) they'll quickly **nail your hat on** (wrap up the deal). You might, on the other hand, be a **stroker** (someone who engages with them for a long time, then walks away without buying). In America this sort of customer is a **beback** (as in 'I'll ...') – hence the saying 'buyers are liars'. In fact while we're in the States, their car sales lingo is way ahead of ours ...

green pea – a new salesman

the point – place on the lot where the salesman stands looking for customers

up – a customer, someone who walks on to the lot

duck on the pond – a customer wandering helplessly around the lot looking at cars

grinder – customer who negotiates hard on price

roach – a customer with a bad credit history

rocket ship – a customer with a high credit rating ('ready for immediate take-off')

one-legger – a husband buying without his wife

quarterback – father or other person brought along by a prospective customer to advise and help negotiate

'the feel of the wheel will seal the deal' – used when urging a test drive

first pencil – opening asking price (unrealistically high)

oddball split – get a compromise figure deliberately wrong – e.g. you're asking $15,000, the customer is offering $14,000 – you say 'Why don't we split the difference and say $14,800?' Customer says 'That isn't a split, $14,500 is a split'. You reply 'OK, so we can have a deal at $14,500?'

Nixon – a complete lie

around-the-block guarantee – one that will only last that long

chicken walk – performed by a car dealer in his TV advert, as he paces up and down in front of his stock

BUSINESS AND FINANCE

BUSINESS AND FINANCE

If you've got the gift of the gab, you might well end up selling things for a living, either in the financial markets or in business more generally. And while you're at it, that same gift of the gab is probably going to generate some jargon along the way ...

The City and Wall Street

Money talks – and so do the people who make it by selling stocks and shares. They have **bed and breakfast deals** (a purchase of stock to be held overnight only) and **concert parties** – groups of people buying shares separately, to use them later as a single holding. They might **clean their skirts** (make final checks before executing a transaction) or, if they have to, **puke** (sell a shareholding at a loss). There are **air-pocket stocks** (shares that are about to collapse) and **drill bit stocks** (ones trading on the New York Stock Exchange at less than one dollar, so that their price is expressed as a fraction similar to those used for drill bits of differing diameters). Other share lingo includes:

ankle-biter (US) – any stock issue with a market value of less than $500 million

Bo Derek (US) – an attractive stock or investment (because in her most famous film she scored a perfect 10)

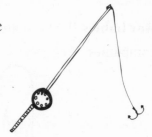

bottom-fishing – buying and selling low-priced (often suspicious) shares

churning – quickly buying and selling an investment to cause market volatility

iceberg order (US) – large order for shares which is split into lots of smaller ones to hide the true quantity being purchased

pump and dump – talk up a share to inflate its price, then sell to make a quick profit (also known as **ramp and de-camp**). The opposite of this is to **short and distort** – talking down a share to reduce its price (also **bash and dash**)

Rio trade – a risky investment that might result in you having to fly away

war babies (US) – shares in defence contracting companies

What sort of investor are you? An **angel** (one who achieves success – if this happens repeatedly you become an **archangel**) or an **Aunt Millie** (what the Americans call an unsophisticated player). Do you **back up the truck** (show your belief in a stock by investing in it on a large scale) or **buy the dips** (purchase stocks whenever they fall heavily in price)? Play it wrong and you'll end up as a **stuckholder** (owner of a share whose price is falling and so can't sell it).

don't fight the tape – don't bet against the way the market is moving

eat well or sleep well (US) – the notion that as an investor you can go for a high or low risk strategy depending on which of the two you want to do

paint the tape (US) – illegally buy or sell a share with collaborators to create artificial market movement (when reported on the ticker tape this will lure in other investors)

quant (US) – someone who uses complex statistical models to predict fluctuations in the stock market

swing for the fences (US) – attempt a hugely ambitious share trade (from baseball, where the phrase means to try and hit the ball over the fence, so allowing a home run)

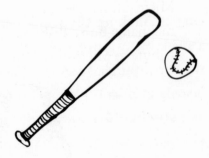

All of this activity can produce **echo bubbles** (small ones that develop after larger ones, caused by investors becoming falsely confident that the market has fallen as far as it can) or a **J-Lo** (a round-bottomed shape to a share's price pattern). A quiet day on the New York Stock Exchange is either a **deer market** (neither a bull nor a bear market, a result of investors being nervous like deer) or a **Valium picnic**.

acquiree – the victim of a takeover

Baby Bells (US) – nickname for the US regional telephone companies formed by the 1984 break-up of AT&T (known as **Ma Bell**). If Microsoft had been forced to break itself up, the nickname **Baby Bills** was ready for use (as a tribute to Microsoft's founder Bill Gates).

big bath – a firm altering its end-of-year figures to seem poorer than it is (**take a bath** can also mean to suffer a loss)

bloatation – an ostentatious or profligate stock market flotation

Chinese wall – information barrier within an investment bank separating those who make investment decisions from others who hold undisclosed information that might influence those decisions (to prevent conflicts of interest)

cut a melon (US) – distribute an additional dividend on top of the normal payment received by shareholders

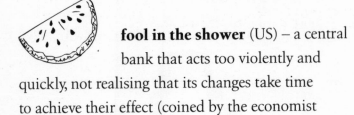

fool in the shower (US) – a central bank that acts too violently and quickly, not realising that its changes take time to achieve their effect (coined by the economist

Milton Friedman, citing a fool who turns the water temperature up or down too much)

foxtrot economy (US) – one whose growth is quick-quick then slow-slow

gap – to delay passing on favourable changes in interest rates

haircut – indication of the amount of borrowing allowed on a corporate bond – if the haircut is 10%, the owner of the bond can borrow 90% of the purchase price

tip from a dip – piece of investment advice from a private source

two and twenty crowd (US) – derisive term for hedge-fund managers, based on their fees (2% of your principal each year, plus 20% of any profits you make)

Money Talks

In the Square Mile, money itself is variously known as **ackers**, **broccoli**, **gelt**, **mazuma**, **rhino** or **Rogan** (... josh – dosh). City traders refer to the yen as the **Bill and Ben**, while in New York the Danish krone is known as the **Copey** (short for Copenhagen)

Specific amounts of money also have their nicknames:

carpet – £3 (or £30, or £300). This dates from the 19th century, and was originally the term for a three-month prison sentence (**carpet bag** – drag, a common name for such a term). Other explanations include the fact that in prison workshops it took 90 days to produce a standard-sized piece of carpet, or that after 3 years prisoners were allowed a piece of carpet in their cell

gorilla – £5

Commodore – £15 (i.e. 'Three Times a Lady' – a **Lady Godiva** being another term for a fiver)

pony – £25. This has its origin in the late 18th century. One explanation is that an Indian 25 rupee note featured a pony, another that it comes from *legem pone*, a phrase meaning 'payment of money, cash down'.

Hawaii – £50 (Hawaii Five-O)

monkey – £500. This piece of slang is roughly the same age as 'pony' – again, possibly because the animal featured on an Indian banknote.

bag of sand – £1000 (grand)

Archer – £2000 (as in Jeffrey's payment to Monica Coghlan)

bar – £1m (from Romany 'bar' or 'bauro', meaning a sovereign)

In the Victorian City of London, a **plum** was £100,000 and a **marygold** was £1m

Business

Office life is a varied life. You can be part of an **adhocracy** (a group that improvises its decision-making) or a **blobocracy** (time-serving middle management). You might encounter **heatseekers** (ambitious colleagues) or **seagull managers** (those who fly in, mess over everything then fly off again). There are **hominterns** (groups of gay contacts adept at business networking) and **wantrepreneurs** (business people operating in the aspirational goods market). Some other terms you might encounter include:

assisted departure – dismissal or redundancy (other such euphemisms being **change of reporting relationship** or **decruitment**)

assmosis – achieving promotion by metaphorically kissing said part of the anatomy

blamestorming – discussions after a disaster in which everyone tries to pin responsibility for it on someone else

blood in the elevator – result of a struggle for control within a firm

camouflage compensation – those parts of the salaries given to senior employees that are kept hidden in publicly available corporate records

chainsaw consultant
– an outsider brought in to
implement redundancies,
leaving the existing
bosses with clean hands

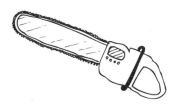

daylighting – working part-time for several different employers

elevator pitch (US) – very brief summary of a proposal (it could be delivered during a ride in an elevator)

funemployment – deciding to use your lay-off as a chance to enjoy yourself

GOOD job – one taken to 'get out of debt'

grey matter – experienced workers taken on by a young entrepreneurial firm in order to appear more established

helicopter view – overview of a topic

lion food – unproductive managers – originated at IBM, where there was a joke about two lions who, escaping from the zoo, split up to increase their chances but agree to meet after two months. When they reconvene, one is skinny and the other overweight. The thin one says: 'How did you manage that? I ate one human and they all started chasing me – I had to hide, and survive on small animals.' The other one replies: 'I hid near an IBM office and ate a manager a day. Nobody noticed.'

NATO – not a team operator

nerd-pack – a row of pens kept in the top pocket

salariat – employees

The physical set up of your office might be known as a **cube farm** (one divided up by partitions), in which case there could be **prairie-dogging** (everyone standing up from their cubicles to see what caused a loud noise). You might eat **al desko** (at your desk – early in the day this will be a **deskfast**), or attend a **topless meeting** (one in which participants are banned from using laptops and other electronic devices, to ensure they concentrate). Or perhaps you'll treat yourself to a **Xerox subsidy** (personal photocopying done at work).

Are you the one in charge of the business? Have you **broken down the silos** (improved the flows of information within your organisation), or **capsized** (set a limit on your staff levels, so jeopardising your business)? Are you **chasing nickels around dollar bills** (concentrating too much on trimming trivial costs when you should be making larger-scale cuts) or **foaming the runway** (desperately investing money in a failing business to try and mitigate the disaster)? Perhaps you've **eaten your lunch** (taken your share of the profits – **eating your breakfast** being to take your share of the profits by moving quickly), and achieved

f*** off money (a quantity sufficient for you to retire)? Other terms to look out for (or avoid) include:

carousel fraud – illegally importing and exporting to avoid (or fraudulently reclaim) VAT

click and mortar – a firm that has both physical stores and an online presence

etail – internet retail

the cockroach theory – any firm announcing bad news will have further faults yet to be disclosed. (Seeing one cockroach is usually evidence that others are nearby.)

kick the numbers – check your data

Kylie – a pleasantly-surprising rise in profits

loading – inflating your end-of-year sales figures

Pac Man – defensive tactic used to prevent a takeover, in which the target firm turns round and launches a bid against the firm trying to buy them

poison pill – a trap set by a vulnerable business to sabotage takeover attempts

sheeple – easily led customers

triple bottom line (3BL) – compiling your accounts to show social and environmental as well as financial factors

wipes its face – an idea that pays for itself

washes its face – an idea that more than pays for itself

SPORT AND LEISURE

SPORT AND LEISURE

We might think it's all about games of two halves and being as sick as a parrot – but sportsmen have far more impressive slang than that. Cyclists **tar surf** (crash), cricketers get **sawn off** (given out incorrectly by the umpire), while basketball players refer to **downtown** (the area furthest away from the basket, where shots count 3 rather than 2 points). If you're involved in American boxing, beware the **Sunday punch** – it's one that knocks you out. And even the bookmakers who make money from sport have their jargon; a **morning glory**, for instance, is a horse that runs better in training than in the race.

Cyclists

If you **caveman it** (ride really hard, also known as **riding eyeballs out**), you might **burger** (crash badly) and get a **gravity tattoo** (a scar). That's why you should never be an **organ donor** (someone who rides without a crash helmet) – what would happen when you **slap your melon on the tarmac** (hit your head on the ground)?

poser exposer – a really steep hill that sorts the good riders from the also-rans

Quad-God – a rider with powerful quadricep leg muscles (the female equivalent is a **Quadess**)

rubberband – the action of sprinting ahead too early, then being caught and overtaken by the other riders

spin and grin – take it easy in a low gear

Tupperware – a composite (plastic) frame

unobtanium – any new alloy used for making bikes, so expensive as to be out of most riders' reach

vulture – to circle at the top of a hill waiting for other riders

Mountaineers

barn door – lose your foot and hand holds on one side of the body (the climber then swings out)

Batman and Robin – pair of climbers who are inseparable

brain bucket – safety helmet

cheese grater – a fall that scrapes the knees, hands and face

chicken wings – the habit of a climber's elbows rising unintentionally when he is tired

drop science – share information

Egyptian – a manoeuvre performed with the body side-on to the rock face

Elvis – to suffer 'sewing machine leg' – when your muscles are under tension and the leg starts shaking

grunt – a very difficult climb

Motorsport

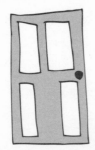

Careful how you **close the door** (steer hard into a corner to prevent the car behind overtaking you) – get it wrong and you might hit the **kitty litter** (gravel at the edge of the track), or even end up in a **worm burner** (crash in which the vehicle slides across a grass verge) or a **T-bone** (crash in which the front of one car ploughs into the side of another at right-angles).

You can drive **balls to the wall** (flat out, also known as **ten-tenths**), though in qualifying you might want to **sandbag** (gain a competitive advantage by deliberately underperforming – from the days when a driver would deliberately brush against sandbags at the edge of the track, so slowing him down and giving him a better starting position. He could then drive at his real ability in the race, claiming he had now learned the track.)

A **Christmas tree** is the series of multi-coloured lights that count down the start to a drag-race (if you start very quickly you're **wired to the tree**), the **meatball** is the flag used to tell a competitor that there is a potentially dangerous fault with his car (it's black with an orange dot in the centre), and the **missing man formation** is used during a pace lap before the race – the vehicle in pole position drops back to the next rank in tribute to a recently-deceased person. **Marbles** are the small pieces of rubber that sheer off the cars' tyres as the race progresses, leaving you with **scuffs** (partly-worn tyres, sometimes used for better handling). In drag racing to **wear the shiny off** is to hit a wall, scraping the paint from your car.

The F1 driver Fernando Alonso, who developed a reputation for escaping blame, has become known by some in the industry as **Teflonso**.

Meanwhile on two wheels, motorcycle racers call their crash helmet their **skid lid** and the passenger seat in a sidecar race the **monkey seat**.

Surfing

You can **hang five** or **hang ten** (surf with the toes of one or both feet extended beyond the edge of the board), though probably not if you're a **shark biscuit** (novice surfer). The foam left after a wave breaks is **soup**.

Golf

Arthur Scargill – a good shot that doesn't get the result it deserves (great strike, bad result)

Sally Gunnell – a mis-hit that sends the ball a long way (not pretty but a great runner)

fried egg – the ball sitting in a hollow in the sand in a bunker

Texas wedge – a putter (because the ground there is so hard and dry you can use that club as a wedge)

American wrestling

The sport revolves around **kayfabe** – the pretence that wrestling is genuine. The term possibly derives from the old days of funfairs, when a **carny** would call home 'collect' (i.e. reversing the charges), telling the operator his name was Kay Fabian. This was code to let his family know he'd arrived safely at the next town – the family would then refuse the call, so avoiding having to pay for it.

Wrestlers engage in **work** (the pre-prepared moves they're given in the script for a match), sometimes to the extent of **juicing** (cutting themselves surreptitiously with a blade concealed in their costume). Get this wrong and they might create a **gusher** (an unintentionally deep wound). Any improvised move not in the script is known as a **shoot.**

face – a wrestler whose character is heroic (short for **babyface**)

heel – a wrestler whose character is villainous

tweener – a wrestler whose character is morally ambiguous (**inbetweener**)

sell an injury – pull out of your next show to convince the audience that your kayfabe injury is real

mark – a fan who believes that the wrestling is genuine

smark – a fan who knows it isn't

canned heat – recorded cheers or boos played over the sound system to artificially create atmosphere

cheap heat – deliberately-created negative reaction from a crowd (for instance by a wrestler wearing a football shirt of the local team's rivals)

potato – to hit or hurt your opponent more than necessary

ring rat – the wrestling equivalent of a groupie

sandbag – to avoid co-operating with a throw, turning yourself into a dead weight, therefore making the throw very much harder to achieve.

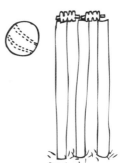

Cricket

No surprise that a sport whose players are widely seen as better-read and more intelligent than, say, the average footballer should produce plenty of jargon. They'll sometimes **play down the Bakerloo when the ball went down the Metropolitan** (just miss the ball – on the London Undergound map those two lines are parallel but slightly apart from each other). They execute **lawnmower shots** (where the bottom hand has to be quickly removed from the bat to avoid a sharply-rising ball, so mimicking the action of pulling a rip-cord) and **washing-line shots** (where the bat is gradually moved away from the body to chase a deviating ball, so copying the feeding out of a looped washing-line).

blob – a duck (score of nought)

buffet bowling – bowling of a quality so poor that the batsman can help himself to runs

bunsen – a pitch suited to spin bowling (**bunsen burner** – turner)

cherry – a new ball, retaining its bright red colour

chin music – succession of short-pitched deliveries aimed at the batsman's head, with the intention of unsettling him

double-teapot – a frustrated bowler/fielder standing with both hands on his hips

fruit salad – spell of bowling where different sorts of deliveries are mixed together to confuse the batsman

Michelle – a haul of 5 wickets in an innings (known by bowlers as a 'five-for', hence the reference to the actress Pfeiffer)

rabbit – a poor batsman (also **ferret** – an exceptionally poor batsman, who goes in after the rabbits)

shirtfront – a very flat pitch, perfect for batting on

Even cricket scorers love their slang. They have **wagon wheels** (charts showing where a batsman scored his runs in a particular innings – with the pitch at the centre, the lines protruding outwards in various directions resemble the spokes of a wheel) and **beehives** (charts showing where a batsman's deliveries have passed him, most of them closely grouped together, resembling bees). There is the **worm** (a graph showing the total number of runs scored against the number of overs bowled, its uneven progress giving the appearance of the bends in said animal), while a **Manhattan** is a vertical bar chart showing the spread of runs throughout a team's innings – the bars of various heights resembling New York's skyline.

American sport

birdcage – the facemask worn by a
lineman in American football

chaingang – the officials who measure out the 10
yards needed to retain possession of the ball

Monday morning quarterback – player who gives
his opinions about strategic decisions after the result
of a game is known

on the numbers – an accurate pass that the receiver
can catch in front of his chest (where the number is
printed on his shirt)

pigskin – the ball

wobbly duck – a badly-thrown pass that veers around
in flight

Meanwhile, also over the pond, baseball players
refer to a ball thrown on a very straight trajectory
as a **frozen rope**, and a batter with an average of

below .100 is said to be **on the Interstate** (American Interstate road numbers are always two digits)

Chess

fish – an inexperienced player

pig – a rook

pigs on the seventh – two rooks doubled on the opponent's seventh rank (also known as **the feeding trough**), in position to take his opponent's pieces and/or trap his king

shot – a strong and surprising tactical move

Gamblers, casinos and bookmakers

It isn't just the tic-tac men's hands that do the talking at the racecourse. A **layer** (bookmaker) at a **bumper** (National Hunt race) will have a **jolly** (favourite horse) and a **rag** (outsider). If he secretly expects the favourite to lose that horse is a **Bismarck** (it'll get sunk), while any horse whose odds are continually shortened because it's being backed so heavily is a **steamer**

beard – someone used to place a bet for someone else

bunny – horse that's a strong favourite (because the bunny always wins a greyhound race) (also **tool**). Such an animal is **nailed-on**

beeswax – rhyming slang for betting tax (also **Ajax**)

blue bet – a false one made to lure unsuspecting punters into copying it

face – a punter with inside information about horses

fiddler – a gambler who lays small bets

kite – a cheque

knock – to avoid paying a debt

nap – a tipster's suggestion for the day's best bet

rock cake – a small bet (a very large one being a **Vesuvius**)

sleeper – uncollected winnings

Z Z Z Z Z Z **under the arm** – untrustworthy

1950s US racetrack slang

If you didn't fancy the **big apple** (a prestigious racing event, especially in New York – this is where the city's nickname came from), you might **beat the bushes** (race your horse at smaller, easier tracks). You'd better not have **dusted your horse** (given it illegal drugs, usually cocaine, to boost its performance), even if it was an **oat muncher** (a horse whose winnings didn't even pay for its food).

A gambler might be a **chalk eater** (one who continually betted on favourites), or have **no show on his shoes** (be trustworthy – he'd been at the track so long there's no way he could have been betting with outside information). Information from inside a stable was **cold dope**, quite possibly about **oil in the can** (a dead-cert horse) or a **gun from the gate** (a fast-starting one). A **blanket finish** was a close one (all the horses could be covered by a blanket), as opposed to one horse winning by a **city block** (a wide margin), in which case it might **finish on the chinstrap** (win so easily it was being restrained as it crossed the line). If the runners **came down like trained pigs** it meant they finished in the order pundits had predicted. A bookie who **dutched a book** had taken bets in such a fashion that he'd lose no matter which horse won the race.

Jockeys who rode in steeplechases (more dangerous than flat races) were the **suicide club**. They were allowed to **go to bat** (whip their horses to make them run faster), but couldn't **spark the horse** (use an illegal **buzzer**, a small electric hand battery). An illegal move in the opposite direction was **sponging your horse** – inserting a sponge in its nostril to reduce its chances of winning (removed immediately after the race). **In the can** was said of a horse not trying to win, while a **midnight handicap** was a fixed race (the outcome being said to have been decided the previous night).

Particular odds have their own names, often derived from the tic-tac signals that go with them. You can back a horse at **wrist** (5/4), **up the arm** (11/8), **ear 'ole** (6/4), **shoulder** (7/4), **double tops** (15/8), **bottle** (2/1) or **carpet** (3/1 – for the explanation of this, see p. 40.) In contravention of standard mathematics, **double carpet** is not 6/1 but 33/1. **Rouf** (pronounced 'roaf') is 4/1 - 'four' spelt backwards. This butcher-like approach (see p. 79) extends to other odds – 7/1 is **neves**, 9/1 **enin** and 10/1 **net**. 100/30, though, relies on rhyming slang: it's **Burlington Bertie**

Meanwhile, in the casino:

action Jackson – a gambler who plays the whole time

fish – the loser at a table. So-named because bad luck is thought to rub off on neighbours as easily as the bad smell from a rotten fish would

rabbit hunting – the futile habit of asking to see what cards would have come up if a hand had continued

Poker players can hold an **Anna Kournikova** (an ace and a king – 'it looks good but rarely wins anything') or a **Harry Potter** – a jack and a king ('JK Rowling')

RETAIL

THE AMERICAN CLOTHING ANTIQUE COINS MARKET TRADERS SLANG MARKET ANTIQUES AUCTIONEERS

RETAIL

Be it the **spray and pray girls** (the women on department store make-up stands who offer free perfume samples), or the traders at London's Smithfield Market with their **dog's eyes** (meat pies) and **Duke of York** (pork), those who sell you things for their living are past masters with the patter.

Nowhere has this tradition been so well-refined as with the word-reversing habit of backslang, invented by costermongers in the 19th century. Instead of asking 'Have you a bit of tobacco?', they'd enquire **'Vatch you a tib of occabot?'**

'Have' became **vatch** because there's no way to pronounce 'h' at the end of a word – so it became 'tch' instead. (It has been pointed out that this is ironic, as Cockney costermongers would drop their 'haitches' at the beginning of a word.) So 'half' became **flatch**, 'hat' was **tatch** and so on.

There was also:

nammow – woman
esclop – policeman
yenep – penny
flatch – halfpenny
yennork – a crown

Yob originated in backslang, though in the Victorian age it was a generic term simply meaning boy

In the 20th century, backslang became the preserve of butchers, and was used to conduct secret conversations in front of unknowing customers. One person who visited a shop in Penge, south London, remembered that just before the First World War, when the butcher saw a certain customer approaching, he would say to his assistant: '**tuck the dillo woc a tib of dillo woc**' — 'cut the old cow a bit of old cow'.

Market traders' slang

As an example of just how localised lingo can get, take a look at these terms used by market traders in Lincolnshire in the 1970s:

blink fencer – trader in spectacles

don't give me the Madame Misharty – don't give me your exaggerated claims/flannel/etc

flim – £5 note

get the clammers on him – don't let him get away without buying anything

give him the bellows – get rid of him

grasshopper – customer who inspects all the goods without buying anything

joint – market-stall

kinger (to rhyme with 'ringer') – a good customer

mushroom – market trader who only appears infrequently (viewed with suspicion by regular traders)

Noah's ark – someone who accompanies a customer and deters them from buying anything

poke-bouncer – someone who uses sleight of hand to look as though he's putting goods into a paper bag, which he then offers for sale

put the essence on – charge excessive prices

Shice McGregor's about today – business is slow

Auctioneers

When the buying and selling is taking place at an auction, a whole new set of jargon comes into play. Merchandise or lots are **kit** (e.g. 'Have you got much kit in at the moment?'), while in America **chant** is the auctioneer's speedy patter. You need to look out for **rings**, groups of dealers acting illegally by agreeing that only one of them will bid on an item they all want, ready for a **knockout** (a second auction held by the dealers among themselves later, to ensure minimal competition and therefore a lower price). A bid that's **on the book** is a commission bid, left in advance by someone who can't attend the auction in person. A **shill** is a fake bid at an auction, made purely to drive up the price, while as the auctioneer you might **take bids off the wall** (pretend that people are bidding when they're not, again just to drive up the price – also known as **bidding off the chandelier**). In America **Statue of Liberty bidding** means keeping your arm raised even before bidding has started, to signify intent. A **snipe**, on the other hand, is a bid placed in an online auction at the last possible moment, leaving other bidders no time to counter.

The dream is a **white-glove sale**, one in which all the lots are sold (an old tradition being that the auctioneer in question was presented with a pair of white gloves). This is also known as a **golden gavel** sale.

Antiques

A shady world, this, one of **rounders** (fake antiques),
wallets (people who fund antiques scams) and
sleepers (stolen antiques that have been deliberately
hidden away until the heat dies down).

carcass trade – faking of old furniture
to make it look antique

cloth job – robbing a church of its antiques

divvy – someone who can spot a quality item when
others are oblivious to its value (short for **diviner**)

flocking – gradually releasing antiques and fakes
claimed to be from the same source

> **honest** – a genuine antique

the match trick – putting two forgeries next to each
other so buyers will assume the better one is genuine

> **sticker** – a shoplifter (also a **shoulder**)

twin – split up a piece of antique furniture, using the
parts to create two pieces, both of which are half-
genuine, half-false

The American antique coin market

There are **bellybutton** dollars (a variety of 1884 silver dollar minted with a defect causing a depression in the eagle's lower abdomen) and the **hot lips** (an 1888 one whose faulty manufacture gave Liberty two sets of lips). The **booby head** was an 1839 large one-cent coin, on which Liberty's face bears an idiotic expression, while the **jackass** is a $10 note issued from 1869 to 1928 – the small eagle at the bottom, when held upside down, looks like a jackass with floppy ears. **Lincoln in a porthole** is a $10 note from the 1920s, containing Lincoln's portrait in a circular frame, and a **three-legger** is a type of 1937 5-cent piece – a set of dies were damaged during use, and in fixing them a technician at the mint accidentally ground off one of the buffalo's front legs. A **blazer**, meanwhile, is any coin in particularly good condition because it was never circulated, or was a proof (also **Godzilla, hard white** or **killer**).

Clothing

The people who dress us have all sorts of tricks up their (and indeed our) sleeves. For instance there's **vanity-sizing** – deliberately labelling a garment with a smaller size than its real one to make customers feel good about themselves. And they know all about the **whale tail** – the top of a G-string protruding above the waistband of someone's trousers.

But the branch of the clothing trade with the richest seam of slang is tailoring. Their lingo has even found its way into the nation's nursery rhymes: a **weasel** (as in 'Pop Goes the ...') was a flat iron used by tailors – the rhyme refers to tailors pawning their irons to go to the pub. An iron with a long curved handle is a **goose**, while a **baby** is a stuffed cloth pad on which cloth is worked. Other equipment includes:

banger – block of wood used when pressing to let the cloth cool whilst keeping it pressed

board – workbench

mangle – sewing machine

mungo – piece of spare cloth used for odd jobs

When it comes to the garments themselves, a **coat** is a jacket (tailors never use the 'j' word), while the part of it that hangs below the waist is the **skirt**. The armhole is the **scye** (short for 'arm's eye'). **Crushed beetles** are badly-made buttonholes, while a **Clapham Junction** is a piece of clothing with lots of additions or alterations made to it. A spoiled job that has to be thrown away is a **kill**, while a garment rejected by a customer is a **pork**. Clumsy working is known as **cutting turf**.

Some slang came from tailors wanting to speak in code in front of the cutters. **On the cod** means 'he's gone for a drink', while **small seams** is a warning called when someone being discussed enters the room.

bast up a snarl – start an argument

being in the drag – being behind on work

boot – a loan until payday (from the days when tailors worked cross-legged and would mark the loan on their sole)

bunce – a tip of some kind (not always cash) given by customer to the tailor or cutter

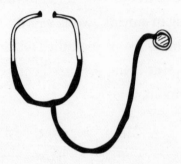

a

cat's face – a small shop opened by a cutter setting up on his own

chuck a dummy – to faint (from a tailor's dummy falling over)

dead horse – a job paid for in advance

doctor – tailor specialising in alterations

drummer – trouser-maker

have a balloon – take a week off without pay

kipper – a female tailor (they used to seek work in pairs to discourage unwelcome advances)

pink a job – complete it with special care

skip it – make stitches too big (known in the East End as **duck shooting**)

skiffle – a job to be completed quickly

tab – fussy customer

trotter – junior who runs work between cutting rooms and tailoring workshops

work by rock of eye – draw and cut by eye, using instinct

A 19th century tailor was a **snip**, **steel-bar driver**, **knight of the thimble** or **Maidstone jailor**, unless he did **sank work** (military tailoring), in which case he was a **stab-rag**. A **springer-up** was a cheap, low-quality tailor, whose clothes would be **blown together.**

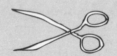

TECHNOLOGY

TECHNOLOGY

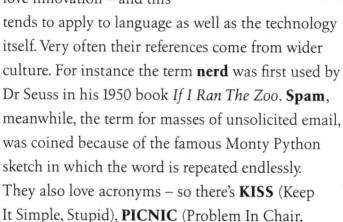

Computer enthusiasts
love innovation – and this
tends to apply to language as well as the technology
itself. Very often their references come from wider
culture. For instance the term **nerd** was first used by
Dr Seuss in his 1950 book *If I Ran The Zoo*. **Spam**,
meanwhile, the term for masses of unsolicited email,
was coined because of the famous Monty Python
sketch in which the word is repeated endlessly.
They also love acronyms – so there's **KISS** (Keep
It Simple, Stupid), **PICNIC** (Problem In Chair,
Not In Computer) and
WOMBAT (Waste Of
Money, Brains And Time).

big iron – a large mainframe computer

chimney wok – a satellite dish

chip jewelry – an old computer destined for scrap

chips and salsa – hardware and software

cobweb – a website that's never updated

crippleware – version of a program partly disabled to allow user to see a partial demo

deep magic – an arcane technique central to a program or system (derived from C. S. Lewis's *Narnia* books)

joe-job – spam forged to look as though it came from an innocent party

frankenputer – computer made up from spare parts of several others (when this is an Apple Mac it's known as a **Hackintosh**)

Computers can of course stop working, run slowly or find other ways of irritating us. They can be **betamaxed** (superseded by new technology), have **mouse droppings** (missing pixels on the screen leaving a small black shape) or exhibit an **angry fruit salad** (a bad font design using too many colours). Programmers occasionally encounter a **banana problem** (not knowing where or when to end a program, from the story of the little girl who said 'I know how to start spelling 'banana', but I don't know when to stop'), or have to use a **bag on the side** (an unsatisfactory extension to an existing program, where a whole new program should have been used – as in colostomy bag). The latter is also known as **ad-hockery**. All this can result in a **bathtub curve** (one that resembles the shape of an antique bathtub, and shows the expected failure rate of a computer system: high at first, dropping to almost zero for most of its lifetime, then rising again as it 'tires out'). The same notion is expressed by **infant mortality** (the theory that most faults with a computer happen near the start of its life).

fritterware – ornate functions on a programme that are unlikely to ever be used

gender bender – cable that alters a male to a female connection, allowing two items of hardware to be linked

goat file – a sacrificial file used to test a computer virus, in other words one carrying a sample of that virus, isolated so it can be studied

honey pot – part of a network deliberately designed to attract and observe hackers (isolated from the rest of the network to ensure safety)

keyboard plaque – the dust and fragments of food that collect between a computer's keys

link-farming – adding weblinks to boost your site's rating (also known as **link incest**)

marching ants – the dotted-line shapes that appear in Photoshop and similar programmes

memory farts – the sound made by a computer when checking its memory on bootup

nipple mouse – the tiny rubber mouse found between the 'g' and 'h' keys on some computers

programming fluid – coffee

Silly Valley – derisive name for Silicon Valley

sock-puppet – false online identity created as part of a fraud

squirt the bird – send a signal up to a satellite

underware – personal files kept on an office network (as opposed to **treeware**, which is a printed book or newspaper)

notwork – a network that has crashed

onosecond – the brief moment in which you realise you've accidentally deleted a whole morning's work

slaptop – a computer whose owner got so frustrated they physically damaged it

Vulcan nerve pinch – simultaneously holding down the CTRL, ALT and DELETE keys, to restart the computer (also **three-fingered salute**)

wave a dead chicken – perform a futile attempt at fixing a computer purely to show willing

Computer operators

What of the people who actually operate computers? Or, as they're sometimes known, the **carbon community** (or **liveware**), who inhabit **meatspace**? You can be a **mouse potato** (someone addicted to the internet – if you're in your teens this makes you a **screenager**), or you can **double-geek** (work on two computers at once). You might suffer **beepilepsy** (a brief seizure when your computer pings to denote a new email), or become a **hacktivist** (a hacker who uses his skills for political protest). The **digerati** are expert users of new technology (as opposed to the **jitterati** – those intimidated by it), who might turn into **entreprenerds** (geeky young IT pioneers, also known as **treps**). **Netiquette** denotes accepted internet customs and procedures, which may or may not include **ego-surfing** (searching the internet for references to yourself). Those working in the American electrical engineering industry have the **Bart's head** (a particular shape of waveform

on a spectrum analyser, which looks like Bart
Simpson's spiky hairdo) and the **Batman**
(another pattern which has high peaks either
side of a flatter section, like Batman's hood with
ears). If you **Bogart** you hog a piece of equipment
that is needed by someone else (similar to spliff-
sharers hanging onto the joint for too long
– inspired by Humphrey Bogart, who used to
smoke a lot in his films), and may have to **go to
the woodshed** (receive a severe telling-off). A
project that's **down to seeds and stems** has run
out of funding (from drug use, where seeds and
stems are all that are left of the stash), while if you
dry-lab you're faking your data (such data being
known as **pidooma** – 'pulled it directly out of
my ass'). To **go open kimono** is to be completely
frank, hiding no secrets, possibly about a **turd in
the punchbowl** (problem). **Milking mice** means
introducing changes that will produce miniscule
benefits, and to **deep six** something is to get rid
of it (from the tradition of burying bodies
at least 6ft deep to stop coyotes digging
them up).

HEALTHCARE

PARAMEDICS
HOSPITAL DYING PATIENTS
DAYS
SLANG
KEEPING THE TRUTH FROM PATIENTS
UNDERTAKERS

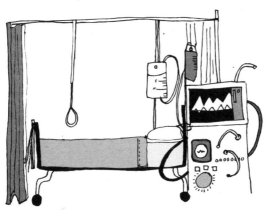

HEALTHCARE

More than perhaps any other profession, doctors and health workers have good reason to employ professional slang. Their stock in trade is illness, disease and death, none of them subjects that lay people – especially the lay people who are suffering those illnesses and diseases, and heading towards those deaths – like to hear about. Yet to do their jobs properly and efficiently, medical workers need to be frank. If a patient isn't going to make it, they have to admit that quickly and move on. It isn't, in their scheme of things, very big news. To the patient, however, it's the biggest news of all. So the doctor needs a way of recording that news quickly and without fuss, allowing another colleague who has more time to communicate it to the patient later on. On notes, therefore, he might write **GPO** – Good for Parts Only.

Also there's the humorous slang that helps doctors and nurses cope with their often challenging working days. Why refer to varicose vein surgery when you

can call it **digging for worms**? Let's load ourselves
onto a trolley, push open those
ward doors and see what
jargon we can find ...

Hospital slang

Had your **bug-juice** (antibiotics)? Then we can
proceed ...

prim – a woman about to give birth to her first child
(short for *primagravida*)

blower – ventilator

whizzer – blood filtering machine

granny dumping – bringing elderly relatives into
hospital just before a holiday

departure lounge – geriatric ward

bury the hatchet – accidently leave a surgical
instrument inside a patient.

brothelizer test – microbiology test to check for sexually transmitted diseases.

supermarket elbow – kid with dislocated elbow from being propelled/dragged around the shops by a parent

Keeping the truth from patients

Have you ever glanced at your medical records across a doctor's desk and been confused by the initials that appear on them? Have you seen a **DIFFC**? Or an **NFN**? If so, it may be time to panic ...

DIFFC – dropped in for friendly chat (i.e. not ill)

NFN – Normal for Norfolk

FLK – Funny Looking Kid

GROLIES – Guardian Reader Of Low Intelligence In Ethnic Skirt

Suffering from **FITH syndrome** – F***ed In The Head

Handbag positive – confused elderly female patient

TTFO – Told To F*** Off. One doctor gave evidence in a court case whose notes included this abbreviation. Asked for an explanation by the judge, he replied: 'To take fluids orally'.

Hasselhoff – patient who gives a bizarre explanation for their injury. (After David Hasselhoff, who claimed to have hit his head on a chandelier while shaving.)

UBI – Unexplained Beer Injury

PGT – Patient Got Thumped

AGA – Acute Gravity Attack (patient fell over)

And it's not just in the NHS where you can hear this sort of thing. Across the pond our American cousins have their own slang ...

pumpkin positive – a patient whose head, if a penlight were shone into their mouth, would light up, thereby revealing its emptiness

3H enema – one that is 'high, hot, and a hell of a lot'

45C – patient who is one chromosome short of a full set (thick)

call button jockey – one making excessive demands on the staff (also **buzzer junkie**)

DBI – Dirt Bag Index (multiply the number of a patient's tattoos by the number of their missing teeth – this gives an estimate of the number of days since they last took a bath)

PFO – Patient Fell Over (while drunk)

Acute Lead Poisoning – gunshot wound

Air-conditioned – multiple gunshot wounds

Dying days

And now the end is near, and so you face a whole new set of jargon ...

albatross – chronically ill patient who remains under the care of a doctor but refuses to actually die

TEETH – Tried Everything Else, Try Homeopathy

rule of five – if patient is hooked up to more than 5 pieces of equipment their condition is critical

cheerioma – a fatal tumour

CTD – Circling the Drain

10th floor transfer (US) – dying (floor number is always the next number on from the highest floor in the hospital)

O-sign – a sign that the patient has died (their mouth is hanging open). If the tongue is sticking out as well it's the **Q-sign**.

patient has moved to Rose Cottage – they've died (also **C/C** – Cancel Christmas)

VSA – dead (i.e. Vital Signs Absent)

Pathology Outpatients – the mortuary

angel lust (US) – a male corpse with an erection (not uncommon)

Mr Post (US) – name used in hospitals to page a morgue attendant when a body needs to be removed from a ward

In case you're becoming offended that healthcare professionals talk this way about those in their care, rest assured that they're just as free and easy with the jargon when it comes to their colleagues ...

Medical workers refer to the **rheumaholiday** department (rheumatology) and the **Freud Squad** (psychiatrists, who are also known as **trick cyclists** and **pest control**), while anaesthetists become **gassers** and surgeons **slashers**.  Intensive Care is the **Expensive Scare Department**, while hospital managers inhabit the **adminisphere** and deal in **administrivia**.

inbred – a doctor whose parents were doctors

ash cash – signing a death certificate used to earn the doctor a fee – and then the body could be cremated (the doctor in this case sometimes referred to as the **gas man**)

MacTilt – the angled head displayed by a Macmillan nurse to convey sympathy

Jack Bauer – a doctor still working after 24 hours on shift

testiculation – a consultant who uses hand gestures while pontificating on a subject they know nothing about

TUBE – Totally Unnecessary Boob Examination

Paramedics

They're first on the scene – and first with the lingo. They either **stay and play** (attend to the injuries themselves), or **scoot and shoot** (send the victim to hospital for more extensive treatment). At the end of every shift paramedics have a **death and doughnuts** meeting, where they discuss the day's cases and unwind. Their nickname for motorbikes is **donorcycles**. In the US an ambulance trip to and from radiation therapy is known as **burn and return**, while a **crispy critter** is a severe burns victim. The team that go out to collect dead bodies from the tracks of New York's subway system are known as **the Pizza Crew.**

Undertakers

Those who deal with the recently bereaved have to be careful with their language. A study in 2007 found that undertakers in Poland were causing offence by using slang terms in front of customers. The word meaning **pendant** was used to describe the body of anyone who was hanged, while **buoy** denoted someone who had drowned.

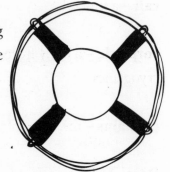

Meanwhile in America undertakers have to be careful who they let hear them talking like this ...

belly puncher – a cavity embalmer. The process entails inserting a tube into the abdomen to release trapped gases, then embalming the corpse.

throat slasher – an arterial embalmer. In this method the body is drained of fluids and then injected (through the neck and other places) with preservatives.

black north – unconsecrated ground where suicides and murderers were traditionally buried, often to the north of the church

bone factory – a hospital or cemetery. The latter is also known as **God's acre** or the **marble orchard**.

call – a funeral

corpsicle – a body frozen for the purpose of cryogenics

cremains – the ashes of a corpse

Death Hilton – a large mausoleum, often a multi-level one

demi-surgeon – an embalmer (the correct term is 'derma-surgeon')

embalmer's grey – a livid pallor on a corpse's face, produced when embalming hasn't been properly carried out

A body that has been put into its **eternity box** or **tree suit** (coffin) has been **potted**, and will then be

planted (buried). If this happens in cold or moist ground the body might then exude **grave wax** (adipocere, a cheese-like substance).

tap the Admiral – to have an alcoholic drink (Nelson's body was preserved in brandy, which his sailors drank as a mark of respect)

thirty – death. This is derived from the old journalistic practice of writing '30' to denote the end of a draft article.

CRIME...

CONFIDENCE TRICKSTERS AND STREET CRIME STEALING GETTING AWAY WITH IT ...OR NOT THE OLDEST... "PROFESSION

CRIME...

Not every way of earning a living is legal. Some people's jobs involve breaking the law – but that doesn't mean that criminals can't have some slang of their own. In fact it appears they've got more slang than most professions. From **twocking** a car (stealing it – the offence is formally known as 'taking without owner's consent') through **loiding** (opening a lock using a strip of celluloid) to the **5-finger discount** (shoplifting), those who step off the straight and narrow certainly have some vivid ways of talking about it.

The language of law-breaking has always reflected the society in which those laws were made. A lot of modern slang, for instance, is about drug dealing. There's the **clocker** (dealer in crack cocaine, because the addict needs it constantly) and the **snowman** (dealer in cocaine/heroin). You can **piggyback** (deal drugs from several floors of a building, so that if one is raided you still have others). The amounts in which you deal might include a **bottle** or a **Janet** (a quarter-ounce, short for **bottle of water** and **Janet Street-Porter** respectively) or even a **Henry** (an eighth of an ounce).

Another modern crime is **shoulder-surfing** (stealing pin numbers at cash-points for use later with copied cards). Back in the 1970s, bank robbers knew their sawn-off shotgun as **nostrils**. Criminals from earlier decades included **Brighton knockers** (door to door con-men) and **anglers** (thieves who used a rod or pole to steal from ground-floor windows).

Sometimes the crimes remain but the language changes. A certain sort of criminal used to be known to the police as a **TGB** (Thieving Gypsy Bastard, a cartoon character in *Viz*). When political correctness kicked in and this was acknowledged as unacceptable, police starting calling such people **stills** (Still a Thieving Gypsy Bastard). A slightly different use of the 'g' word was common in the 1990s: **gypsy's warning**. This meant having a quiet word in a young miscreant's ear, and dated back to the days when naughty children were told they'd be taken away by gypsies.

Stealing

People have always wanted to help themselves to others' property. In the 16th century a thief was a **prig** (a **bawdy basket** being a female thief). A hundred years on you could **nim** (steal) using a **betty** (a burglar's jemmy), while in the 18th century a **badger** was someone who robbed and murdered near rivers, a **glazyer** was a burglar who broke or removed windowpanes, and a **morning-sneak** was an early-morning robbery committed by creeping in while the domestic servant was cleaning the front doorstep. Other terms down the ages have included:

heave a cough – rob a house

going upon the dub – robbing a house by picking the locks

mill a glaze – break a window

shutter-racket – rob a house by boring a hole in the shutter then breaking the window

towline – robbery committed by enticing a person out of their premises with a fictitious story, then having your acquaintance go in and steal their possessions

fagger – a small boy passed through the window of a house to open the door from the inside

lully prigger – a thief who took clothes from washing lines

trig – a piece of paper or small stick placed by a thief in the keyhole of a house which they think might be uninhabited – if it was there the next day the thief would know they could enter and rob the place

hoister – shoplifter

spank a glaze – rob a shop by smashing its window and grabbing something on display, having first tied the door handle on the outside to prevent the shopkeeper coming out to catch you

give it to a shopkeeper upon the mace – obtain goods from him on credit with no intention of paying

bleating rig – the practice of stealing sheep

dromedary – a bungling thief

poulterer – a thief who opened mail and took the money from it

sword racket– taking money by enlisting in several army regiments then deserting from all of them (also known as **pear-making**)

snaffling lay – highway robbery (a **high-toby** being a highway robbery committed on horseback)

water-sneak – act of robbing a vessel on a river or canal by boarding it unseen at night

Confidence tricksters and street crime

In the 18th century you could **cross-fam** (pick a pocket by crossing your arms in a particular way), **bishop** or **christen** a watch (replace its name and number with a false one to prevent it being traced) or **run smobble**  (snatch goods off a counter and throw to them to an accomplice, who ran off with them). To deceive someone was to **bam** (from bamboozle) or **kimbaw** them, possibly by **dropping a cog** (letting fall a piece of gold or silver in order to draw in and cheat someone who sees it), or **drawing the king's picture** (producing counterfeit currency). A **figure dancer**, meanwhile, was a forger who altered the numbers on banknotes. Other historical terms have included:

Abraham-man – someone who worked as a beggar by pretending to be insane (named after the Abraham ward in London's Bedlam lunatic asylum)

coney-catcher – a con artist ('coney' meaning rabbit)

martin – the victim of a con-trick

diver – a pickpocket

Jason's fleece – gold pieces offered to entice victim into buying fake gold (Jason stole the Golden Fleece)

Pickpockets (or **forks**) might **spring a partridge** (draw a crowd for the purpose of picking their pockets). To **clout** was to concentrate on picking handkerchiefs, while to **stall up** was to surround a victim, usually in a crowded place such as a theatre entrance, forcing his arms up so that he couldn't defend his pockets. If the pickpockets **knuckled** they had worked in an expert manner – any less skilled operation was known as **buzzing**.

The victim in a card-game con trick was the **cousin**. He would be approached by the **setter** or **taker-up**, shortly followed by the **verser**. These two would get his confidence, then be joined by the **barnard** or **barnacle**, someone pretending to be drunk or stupid. The setter and verser would then encourage the cousin to play cards with the barnard, who would inevitably win. (If someone was needed to create a diversion in this con he was known as the **rutter**.)

burn a ken – leave an alehouse without paying your bill

cat and kitten rig – the practice of stealing pewter quart and pint pots from pubs

fawney rig – a brass ring, gilted to look like gold, sold as the real thing

philliper – thief's accomplice who kept a lookout for the police

queer-soft – counterfeit coins, also known as **sheen** or **sinkers**

In the 20th century, meanwhile, you might **burn the town** (work a crime all over a town until you had to move on to another), then **take a powder** (disappear quickly). To **buzz** was to distract someone's attention while your colleague picked his pocket (**on the buzz** meaning pickpocketing), while **kite-flying** was passing forged cheques.

Terms from a Victorian street beggars' map, showing tips on how to operate in different areas:

bone – good

cheese your patter – don't talk much here

cooper'd – spoilt by too many tramps calling there

gammy – unfavourable

flummuxed – dangerous, sure of a month in **quod** (prison)

Getting away with it...

bonnet – cover story (such as a conventional job) used to cover the proceeds of your crimes

flash ken – a house that harboured thieves

get your money at the best – to live by dishonest practices

row in the boat – to take a share of the proceeds of a crime

stalling ken – premises of a receiver of stolen goods

stophole abbey – meeting place for thieves

oaken towel – a cudgel

to put someone in the garden – to defraud a fellow thief of his share of the proceeds of a crime

...or not

whittle – to confess on the gallows

nubbing-cove – a hangman

shoulder-clapper – a policeman

The oldest profession

As you might expect from a crime that's been around so long, prostitution has a whole host of terms associated with it. In the 16th century it was the **loose-coat game**, in the 19th century it was **fancy work**, and by the 1930s it had become **bashing**. Over in America you might **sling fish**, while down in Australia you would **crack it for a quid**.

Perhaps the most productive era for jargon in this country was the 19th century. Prostitutes were said to **carry a broom at the masthead** (it was a naval

tradition that a ship which had been sold did this), **flutter a skirt**, **go sparrow-catching**, **hawk their mutton**, or **tread their shoe awry**.

While touting for business they would ask a man **'Are you good-natured?'** An enquiry the other way round would involve the man asking a woman if she was **gay**. The prostitute would reply that yes, she was **unfortunate**. If she wasn't a prostitute, the woman would fail to understand the question and so the man would avoid offending her.

Not that the parties involved have always been so coy with their language. From the **fly-boats** of the 1700s to the **daffodils** of the mid-20th century, working girls (and boys) have always been ready with the slang. In the 16th century you would be a **pinnace**, a **carvel**, or **traffic**. A **mort wap-apace** was an experienced prostitute (it means 'girl f***-fast'), and a **green goose** a young prostitute. Shakespeare uses the word **strumpet** for prostitute in more than a dozen plays.

By the 1800s terms included **laced mutton, plover**, **Whetstone Park deer** and **buss beggar** (an old prostitute, a buss being a kiss). Come the Victorian era, the profession's slang had multiplied even further. A prostitute might be known as a **jack's delight** (a **jack tar** being a sailor), a **Fulham virgin**, a **trat** ('tart' in backslang) or a **pinchcock**. There was also **ladybird**, **buttock** and **mott. Brass** also originated around this time (brass nail – tail). A **hedge whore** was a lowly prostitute, a **kid leather** a young one, a **dasher** a flashy one and a **toffer** a high-class one. A **dollymop** only worked part-time, a **three-penny upright** charged for sex against a wall, and a **wasp** was infected with venereal disease. Other Victorian terms included **cab** or **pheasantry** for a brothel, possibly overseen by an **abbess** (a female brothel-keeper). Frequenters of such establishments were **Corinthians**.

Modern slang from America includes **lot lizard** (a prostitute who frequents truck-stop parking lots), **ginger** (one who steals a client's money) and **flat-backer** (one who has sex with a lot of clients).

It isn't only women who practice the profession, of course. Gay male prostitutes have over the years been referred to as ...

minion of the suburbs (16th and 17th centuries)

mandrake (Victorian)

burton ('Burton-on-Trent', 1960s and 70s)

boulevard boy (1970s onwards)

buff boy (20th century)

dilly boy (young male prostitute working around Piccadilly Circus)

maud (1940s onwards)

aspro (US)

Susan Saliva (US, 1950s–70s) – male prostitute specialising in fellatio

Pimps, meanwhile, have down the centuries been known as **mutton tuggers**, **knights of the gusset**, **pensioners to the petticoat** and **Haymarket hectors**. 20th century rhyming slang made them **fish and shrimp**, while in Yiddish they were a **shundicknick**. In the 16th century a pimp was a **picked-hatch captain** – the picked-hatch (a spiked half-door) was used as the sign of a brothel, and **to go to the manor of picked hatch** meant to visit a brothel (it's said by Falstaff in *The Merry Wives of Windsor*). In America a pimp might be a **nookie bookie**, or (in black slang) he'll **work from a book**. A **lighthouse**, meanwhile, is a person who directs customers to a bar where prostitutes can be found.

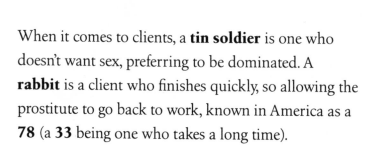

When it comes to clients, a **tin soldier** is one who doesn't want sex, preferring to be dominated. A **rabbit** is a client who finishes quickly, so allowing the prostitute to go back to work, known in America as a **78** (a **33** being one who takes a long time).

Other American terms include the **Boston tea party** (the prostitute urinating on the customer) and **going below 14th Street** (the client performing oral sex on the prostitute, such a customer being a **bennie**). To **Georgia** is to refuse to pay a prostitute after having sex with her. On the other hand the prostitute can do a **cash and dash** – take the client's money then run. Another scam is the **bait and switch** – advertising with a picture of a girl other than the one a client will end up seeing. A condom is a **beret** or an **umbrella**. Some transvestite prostitutes use a **gaff**, a special g-string that hides their genitals.

... AND PUNISHMENT

...AND PUNISHMENT

If your nefarious deeds go wrong, and you come to the attention of the authorities, a whole new set of slang comes into play. You can **go bandit** (plead not guilty), unless the police **burst** you into a **cough job** (a confession). Either way you'll find yourself up before the **three monkeys** (a magistrates' bench), and possibly doing **bird** (time in prison – **bird-lime**). But it isn't just those on the receiving end of justice who employ jargon – let's start with those whose job it is to catch the criminals ...

The police

They can **spin a drum** (perform a search of a property) or carry out a **nut and gut** – (medical examination). Sometimes the boys in blue carry out **contact therapy** (restrain someone physically), possibly with an **Alabama lie detector** (term imported from the USA for a police baton, also known as **Mr Wood**). In America they can arrange a **perp walk** – parading an accused person (i.e. accused of being a perpetrator) through a public space, supposedly as a way of transporting them to or from court, but in reality to allow the press to take photos of them.

But the police don't just have slang relating to criminals – they talk about the public using jargon too ...

100 yard hero - a member of the public who shouts obscenities at a police officer from a safe distance

'Do you take warrant card?' – asking a publican/ shopkeeper etc if they give police officers goods for free

innit – a chav

a three – a black person (from IC3, part of the police's racial grouping codes – these go up to IC6 – **IC7** is unofficial slang for a ginger person)

window licker – a deranged or psychotic person

And Her Majesty's Constabulary have more than a few terms relating to themselves. A **black rat** is a traffic officer, unpopular with the rest of the police; this refers to the fact that the black rat eats its own young. (It's alleged that traffic officers put black rat stickers in the backs of their cars to avoid being pulled over by colleagues.) A **black rover**, on the other hand, is a warrant card, when used as a travel card on bus, train or London Tube services (police get free travel within a certain radius of their home town). A useless or lazy officer is variously a **clothes hanger**, a **BONGO** (Books On Never Goes Out), an **Olympic torch** (never goes out), **station cat** or **Ghurkha** (doesn't take prisoners). In a van he might well occupy the **BINGO seat** (the one at the back, the term being short for Bollocks I'm Not Getting Out).

A **Blunkett babe** is a Police Community Support Officer (established by that politician when Home Secretary), or a **C3PO**, or possibly a **CHIMP** (Can't

Help In Most Police situations). The **choirboys** are HM Revenue and Customs (also known as **Lillywhites**), while the fire brigade is **Trumpton**. The **Kremlin** is New Scotland Yard (also known as **Cowards' Castle**).

Your **turtles** are your gloves ('turtle doves'), **hats and bats** are helmets and riot sticks, and a **stinger** is a set of spikes laid across the road to puncture tyres of an escaping vehicle

Other terms include:

butterfly – officer who engages in lots of activity (usually unproductive) and gets promoted

canteen cowboy – officer who likes to advise other officers

CV job – case leading to a lot of convictions

DILLIGAFF – Does It Look Like I Give A Flying F**k?

first aid kit – evidence kept ready to plant on someone

gunship – unmarked car carrying armed police

lids – uniformed officers

Not Carnival Related – a complete lie (from the police denying that an incident in Notting Hill was connected to the carnival)

onion – sergeant (i.e. 'onion bhaji')

show out – give subtle hints when stopped that you are also a police officer

station stamp – coffee mug stain on a statement

Bobbies came to be slang for police because the force was instigated by Robert Peel, while the metal from which their badges were made inspired the name **copper**.

(Another explanation cites the ferrules on their canes.) Meanwhile William IV's constables, who functioned as an early form of police, are said to have given rise to the term **Old Bill**.

At road traffic accidents, a **FUBAR BUNDY** is a victim who is 'F***ed Up Beyond All Repair, But Unfortunately Not Dead Yet', while **DODI** means 'Dead One Did It' (said of a solo-vehicle incident, e.g. crashing into a tree).

Courtroom slang

Criminals' vocabularies widen considerably when they reach court. They stand in the **Brighton** (Rock – dock), and listen to the **garden** (gate – magistrate) or **Barnaby Rudge** (judge), or possibly the **bubble and squeak** (beak – also **once a week**). In the 19th century a **milky beak** was a drunken magistrate, while a **rum beak** was one who could be bribed (a **queer beak** being one who couldn't). As you awaited trial you were **in for patter** (that of the barristers and the judge). In 1940s New York the judge was **the man with the book of many years.**

Lawyers, according to Victorian criminals, were **sons of prattlement**, **mouthpieces** or **jaw coves**. (An incompetent one was a **puzzle-cause**.) In the 20th century your lawyer was your **tongue.** In the US, criminals call some lawyers **dump trucks** – those (appointed at public expense) known for making life easy for themselves by getting their clients to plead guilty.

Barristers have their **rat's tails** (the little strands hanging down at the back of their wigs), and operate not from chambers but from **sets**. A **white wig** is a new barrister. (A senior QC's wife once had his wig cleaned for him as a surprise – he was horrified, saying 'It took 20 years to get my wig looking like that!') Your **call** is the year that you were called to the bar (qualified as a barrister) – so someone will be, for instance, a **2003 call**. Speaking of a veteran barrister people will say **'He's 30 years called'**. In Australia, QCs, commonly known (as in Britain) as **silks**, are sometimes referred to dismissively as **rayons**.

Barristers' clerks talk of a **Dionne Warwick** (a distressing event, Warwick having had a hit called *Heartbreaker*), a **drilldown** (conversation with a verbose barrister listing several things to be done when you have no pen or pencil to hand) or a **bomb** (an entry in your diary that causes you alarm). After any of those you might need a **frightener** (an alcoholic drink).

In Victorian times barristers were known as **blue bags** (after the item in which they carried their papers – these bags are still used today). A QC was a **red bag**. To **go into the rope-walk** meant to take up practice in the Old Bailey (the ways of London lowlife were called **the ropes**, and to **know the ropes** meant to be familiar with them). Your brief (collection of papers relating to a case) was your **soup** (they enabled barristers to eat). A **snipe** was a lawyer who presented a long bill.

Modern solicitors refer to **killer bees** (aggressive lawyers) and **mezzanine partners** (those whose pay and conditions are slightly less favourable than those of the senior partners). The select group of the most prestigious law firms is known as the **magic circle**. If a non-lawyer (typically a senior executive) **wears trousers** it means a lawyer can meet and negotiate with him without that person's own lawyer being present. The implication is that the executive's trousers prevent him being metaphorically 'interfered with' by the lawyer. Libel lawyers have the **small**

penis rule, a ploy used by writers in avoiding libel suits – a character in a novel is given an undesirable characteristic (such as said physical attribute) to prevent anyone coming forward and claiming the character is based on them.

In America, a **whippy** is a compensation claim relating to a whiplash injury, and an **apology law** is legislation allowing medical professionals to express sympathy to a patient who suffered injury in hospital, without admitting liability. Lawyers might be **frantastic** (pretending to be busier than they really are, to avoid being given any more cases to work on) or engage in **lawfare** (launching a legal case against an opponent purely with intention of damaging them or tying up their time).

The jury is the **tomato** ('purée'), as opposed to a **banana**, which is a bent policeman, not to be confused with a **bender** (a suspended sentence). Police in their turn refer to **dock asthma** – the fake gasp of astonishment from a defendant in court when confronted with the accusations against him.

Barristers refer to a **booty sentence** (a harsh one), and can **carve a trial** (do a deal, agreeing that their client will plead guilty to, say, three charges in exchange for another two being dropped), or **crack a trial** (persuade their client to plead guilty in exchange for a lesser sentence). They might try to **robing room** (intimidate) their opponent ('I'm not trying to robing room you or anything, but I can't see your chap has a defence to this one – is he going to do the decent thing and plead?') A barrister speaking in court is said to be **on his feet**.

American lawyers might use a **SODDI defense** (one in which the defendant admits that a crime occurred but that he wasn't responsible for it, i.e. 'Some Other Dude Did It'), or, if the defendant names a particular person as the criminal, a **TODDI defense** (That Other Dude Did It).

The **unicorn defense** means blaming another (mythical) person for the crime, the **aw shucks defense** has the defendant pleading confusion or lack of intelligence, and the **ostrich defense** is one in which a senior member of an organisation claims that they cannot be expected to know everything that was being done by those under their command.

Other terms used by US lawyers include:

CSI effect – the process whereby jurors have come to expect more forensic evidence than is actually necessary to establish guilt. So common that potential jurors are now asked about their television-watching habits during jury selection.

habe – an appeal against unlawful imprisonment (from *habeas corpus*)

Philadelphia lawyer – one who knows the law in minute detail. Derives from Andrew Hamilton, a lawyer from that city who successfully defended a newspaper publisher charged with libel.

pseunonymous – the status of a witness who gives evidence under a permitted false name so as to preserve their anonymity

soup-spitter – a young, irritating but essentially harmless criminal

spit and acquit – process by which a drug defendant can go free if they agree to provide a DNA sample

testilying – giving false evidence

unring the bell – phrase used to describe the impracticality of a judge asking a jury to forget information which has come out in court but which is inadmissible – 'You can't unring the bell'

wagon-chasing – similar to ambulance-chasing – following a police wagon back from the scene of arrest to the police station to offer to represent the arrested person

Australian lawyers refer to **hot tubbing** – opposing expert witnesses being forced to give their evidence together, so allowing the judge to arrive at his conclusion more quickly.

You are hearby sentenced...

It's what you might call the 'business end' of the trial. Criminals know the sentences that various crimes can attract: back in the 18th century they spoke of a **lagging matter** (any crime for which the punishment was likely to be transportation) and **working under the armpits** (committing only those crimes which would attract a non-capital punishment – the noose being applied above the armpits).

To keep an ironmonger's shop meant to be hung in chains, but some of the most vivid slang was reserved for the harshest sentence a court could pass. You could **climb a ladder to bed** or **ride a horse foaled by an acorn**. The sentence of death was known as the **cramp word**, while the gallows themselves were the **deadly nevergreen**, the **Gregorian tree**, the **three-legged mare**, the **sheriff's picture frame** or the **morning drop**. Being hanged was known as **dying of hempen fever**.

Early 20th century American criminals knew the electric chair as the **frying pan**, the **humming bird**, or the **squativoo** (from *squattez-vous*, cod-French for 'sit down'). Nowadays it's sometimes called the **barbeque stool**. Being hanged is **doing the air dance**, a similar term to the one used at Spandau prison, where Nazi war criminals were executed: the **Spandau ballet** (hence the name of the 1980s British pop band). A lethal injection is the **big jab** or the **stainless steel ride**.

Prison slang

Are you a **fish** (a first-time prisoner)? You might not know that **jam roll** is parole, that the **bone yard** is the area used for overnight visits of wives/girlfriends, or that **catching a ride** is asking someone with drugs if they can spare you some. If you **get on the dummy** you refuse to grass on someone (also known as **holding your mud**), while the **Pepsi Generation** are younger prisoners who lack respect for old-timers.

A **tailor made** is a conventional (as opposed to hand-rolled) cigarette – a luxury in prison – and to **keister** (pronounced 'keester') is to hide something in your rectal cavity (also known as **the suitcase**). Prison guards are known, amongst other things, as **hacks**, **hogs**, **pigs**, **snouts**, **cops** or **bulls**. The most famous term for them, **screws**, is said to come from the time when a guard would turn a screw to make the prison treadmill more punishing.

The authorities, in their turn, refer to **Hobbits** (prisoners who comply with the system) and **gate fever** (the emotion shown by a prisoner nearing the end of his sentence). The tag worn by criminals on release from prison is the **Peckham Rolex**.

When an American criminal **hits the pit** (gets sentenced to time in prison), he will be transferred to the **Crossbar Hotel** (it used to be the **concrete womb**), unless the criminal is a woman, in which case she goes to the **hen pen**. Being in prison is being **on ice**. **All day and night** is a life sentence (also known as **doing the book**), **Buck Rogers time** is a sentence so long your release date is unimaginably far in the future, while **killing your number** means completing your sentence. This is easier if you've been given **wino time** (a short sentence), which you may have been if you're a **butterfly** (a young and attractive prisoner).

You'll **go to the boss** (be searched by the Body Orifice Security Scanner, a hi-tech chair that acts as a metal detector, alerting the authorities to, for example, SIM cards smuggled inside someone's body), then progress to a cell where your **fart sack** (bed) awaits. If you're gay you might be put in the **daddy tank** (a segregated block used to protect homosexual prisoners from other inmates). Your **bean chute** is the slot through which food trays are inserted, possibly bearing **erasers** (chunks of processed chicken).

Things don't always run smoothly. There might be a **bingo** (prison riot), a **blanket party** (said item being thrown over a despised prisoner prior to assaulting him, so he won't be able to identify the attackers) or someone could be **dressed out** (assaulted with urine or excrement).

Other terms from American prisons include:

border brothers – Mexicans

bump your gums – talk excessively

cho-mo – someone serving time for child molestation (also **pamper pirate** or **diaper sniper**)

cop a heel – escape from prison (also known as **jackrabbit parole**)

diesel therapy – to keep transferring a prisoner, so preventing him associating with others for too long

drop a dime – inform on someone

dry rat – a prisoner who informs on someone in front of another person

duck – an officer who passes information to prisoners about fellow officers

high class – hepatitis C (while HIV is known as **the Monster**)

marble orchard – prison cemetery (established because the bodies of many long-term prisoners aren't claimed by anyone)

sweat the fence – dream of escaping

talk on the pipe – conduct a conversation with prisoners in other cells via the plumbing system, achieved by both of you placing pillows on your toilet and jumping up and down, so creating a plunger effect and forcing the water out – this leaves the pipes empty and capable of carrying sound

MEDIA

JOURNALISTS
TV NEWS
PHOTOGRAPHERS
THE BOOK TRADE
ADVERTISING

 # MEDIA

You'd expect the media – people who work with language for a living – to have created a whole raft of slang for the things they do and the ways they do them. And you'd be right. From journalists and their **nibs** (very short items of news, short for 'News in Brief') to advertisers and their **worship shots** (the ones that linger on the product, showing it in all its glory), the inhabitants of Meejah Village just love a bit of jargon ...

Journalists

The common term for journalist is **hack**, though they occasionally call themselves **scribes** or even **blunts** (as in pencil). (Hack comes from **hackney scribbler**, a 17th century term for a jobbing writer. Around that time **Grub Street news** meant false news.) In America they're known as **ink-slingers** or **pencil-shovers**, and the newspapers they produce are **blatts**; tabloids are **tabs** while broadsheets are **heavies**. (When the editor of *The Sun* in Britain, Kelvin MacKenzie used to refer to them as **the unpopulars**).

dead tree edition – paper copy (as opposed to online edition) of a newspaper

anecdata – unscientific, informally-gathered statistics used in an article

griff (US) – accurate information

sob-sister (US) – female journalist who specialises in sentimental stories

Journalists' love of death and disaster is summed up in their saying '**if it bleeds it leads**'

cereal test (US) – editor's judgement as to whether a story is appropriate to publish (can you imagine people reading it at the breakfast table?)

journalese – expressions/style of writing in vogue with journalists at a particular time

reviewphemism – kind or libel-proof way for a reviewer to criticise a book, a play etc. (e.g. 'wears its scholarship lightly' means badly-researched)

advance – news story about an event yet to happen

The well-known verb **to doorstep** (to appear outside someone's front door in search of their comment) has now made its way to the civil service, who have turned it into a noun – they arrange **doorsteps** for politicians, informal press conferences on the street

envelopmental journalism (US) – a journalist being bribed (given money in an envelope) to write a favourable story

buy-up – a payment made to someone with a story to tell. People who have been **bought up** are often **babysat** by reporters to stop them leaking information to rivals.

bulks – free copies given out for promotional purposes

How a newspaper is actually produced

In a newspaper office, reporters sit on **desks**, as do the news staff, but sub-editors, for some reason, sit at **tables**. The **copy tasters** are people who sit on the news desk and act as the first filter system, weeding out weak stories, while the **back bench** is the table of very senior production people who help decide what goes where and write the main headlines. Journalists file **copy**, **stories**, **tales** or **pieces** – never articles.

splash – the main story on a newspaper's front page

hamper – the story across the top of the front page on a broadsheet (also **attic**)

basement – the story along the bottom

sub-deck – a secondary headline underneath the main one (e.g. If 'Stock market plunges 5%' is the headline, 'Investors in rush to sell' would be the sub-deck)

par – a paragraph (no journalist ever uses the full word – though they will sometimes say '**graf**')

wob – a headline which has been reversed so that it's white on black, for extra dramatic effect

starbursts – words or phrases surrounded by stars for added visual impact ('summer sizzler' or the like)

kicker – the opening lines of a story in a different font to grab attention

furniture – collective name for the fact boxes, pictures, and so on that break up the text of a story

puff-box – fact box set within a story – at BBC News Online these became known as **mega-puffs**, and then as they developed further, **hyper-puffs**

bang – an exclamation mark (also **screamer** or **dog dick**)

pull-out – quote from a story displayed within it to grab readers' attention

A piece may or may not get a good **show** in the paper. This may be **front-of-book** (towards the front of the paper). Further on will be **think pieces** (articles reflecting on events in the news), possibly on the **op-ed** pages (those opposite the editorials). Those in charge of the obituary pages will often **tickle an obit** (make minor changes to the piece on a major figure). These appear near **hatches, matches and dispatches** (the birth, marriage and death announcements).

stale – the opposite of a scoop, in other words a story that every paper has. A hack's nightmare is a **miss** – not having a stale that everyone else has got. In this case you have to file a humiliating **catch-up**.

ferret – changing the layout of the newspaper at the last moment when a big story breaks. The term dates from Kelvin MacKenzie's time as editor of *The Sun*, and is based on the idea that he was sticking a metaphorical ferret up his journalist's trouser-legs. To make a further change to the layout was known as a **reverse ferret**. This term has subsequently come to mean a sudden about-turn in a paper's editorial stance.

Evening papers have slang to denote their different editions throughout the day – on the *London Evening Standard* this used to be **stars**. The **one star** would be the earliest edition, all the way through to the **five**

star, the latest. The papers would actually have these number of stars printed on them, even though they would also have labels such as 'Late Prices Extra' or 'West End Final'.

kill fee – paid to a journalist when an article isn't used

Photographers

The men and women behind the lenses are as handy with the lingo as they are with a flashgun ...

smudge – photo (or a **collect**)

Photographers are **snappers**, or occasionally **monkeys** (because they climb trees to get a good vantage point). They **ping** pictures back to the office. In the past if one of them (possibly on a doorstep) had missed a picture they would **blag a neg**(ative) from one of the others.

goat f*** – the scramble of photographers at the back of a media scrum as they try to get a picture. Some may resort to a **Hail Mary** (taking photos by holding the camera above their head instead of looking through the viewfinder).

hose the Doris – take rapid multiple photos of a female celebrity

shotgun (US) – take lots of shots in quick succession

monster – jump out from behind a bush or other object to deliberately shock a subject, thereby making them look unattractive or suspicious in the photo

gun – flash (but in America it means the camera – a flash is a 'lamp')

soup (US) – film developer

sticks – tripod

jar – lens (also **pot**, and in America it's a **glass**)

mortar – long lens (also **stinger** and **beercan** in the US)

chimping – constantly checking the display of your digital camera (seen as unprofessional) (also **pixel peeping**)

cross-chimping – comparing your shots to those of other photographers

grip'n'grin – the quick handshake shot posed by politicians, at awards ceremonies, etc

Non-journalistic photographers will sometimes achieve a photograph that's **sooc** – so good it doesn't need to be retouched (straight out of camera).

Photographers are known to fashion models as **togs**

velvet fiddler – a fussy portrait photographer

TV news

You know those headlines at the beginning of a TV news programme? They're **bongs** (from the old *News at Ten* programme, which used Big Ben's chimes in its opening). **Goldfishing** means having a speaker or interviewee in vision but not hearing their voice (avoided at all costs), while a **lockout** is the bit at the end of a report where the correspondent says 'This is John Smith, at the Old Bailey, for ITN News'. Reporters also use the **noddy** (shot of them nodding to the interviewee's answers) and the **walkie-talkie** (interview conducted as both parties walk along, in an attempt to make it look more interesting). A **WDIAM** (pronounced 'wuddiam' and standing for 'What Does It All Mean?') is the part of the report where a specialist correspondent sums up what's really behind the story. Back in the studio, American programmes might have a **roboanchor** – a newsreader who reads but does not understand the news.

The book trade

Publishing slang is evolving to take account of new technology. A **blook** is a book based on a blog, while a **flook** is a film based on a blook. All a long way from the 17th century, when there was only the printed page, and **top-dressing** meant using a well-known writer to provide a preface to a new writer's work.

The printer's job is one of those that's on the cusp of disappearing in the age of the internet – but while they were around they had some great slang ...

printer's pie – the mess made by dropping a load of lead type

sling type – to set or compose the type

A **hell box** was one containing unused type (quite possibly **squabble** – type that had got mixed up)

fat – blank space on a page, for which a printer was paid at the same rate as a full page (hence **fat** came to mean 'easy to compose', **lean** being the opposite)

brains – the paste used by a sub-editor to stick cuttings together

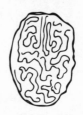

chalk your pull – things are on hold

shriek – an exclamation mark (also **admiration**)

One printer's term found its way into wider usage. **Sorts** were the letters of the alphabet – to be **out of sorts** meant your type-case was lacking them. This is where we get the modern phrase meaning 'unwell'.

19th century printers' slang

Back then, a printer was known as a **typo**. They sometimes worked in **cock-robin shops** (small firms employing inexperienced workers on low wages). On entering a new firm you had to pay a **benvenue** (a fee to the trade union chapel, derived from *bienvenue*, French for 'welcome'). A compositor was often known as a **galley slave**.

Equipment included the **donkey**, a subsidiary engine used in addition to the main one. (Helicopter pilots also call their engine their donkey). A **coffin** was the carriage or bed of a cylindrical press, while **fugitive colours** were inks that were not permanent, and so faded on exposure. **Bottle-arsed** described type that was thickened at the bottom through wear and tear and/or incorrect planing down (**bottle-necked** was thicker at top) and **foxed** paper was stained or mouldy. Also on animals: **horse** meant charging on account of work that had not yet been finished, while a **pig** was a journalist (compositors were the first to call Fleet Street's finest by this name – the journos responded by calling compositors **asses**).

Balaam was sets of pages of spare feature articles that were set and kept ready for use when a newspaper space would otherwise be blank, while in a book the **bastard title** was a half-title before the full title of a work.

A **pos** was an apostrophe, and **cock-up** described a superior figure or letter (such as the r in M^r).

Printers knew how to play as well as work. **Jeff** meant to gamble using quadrats (metal spaces of various sizes used for filling up short lines) as dice. If one quadrat landed on top of another it was called **cock**, and another throw was allowed. Meanwhile **G.I.** was a celebration, for instance of a birthday (short for general indulgence). Too much of that and you'd indulge in **Ms and Ws** (a drunk person's unsteady gait). **Ps and Qs**, on the other hand, were what novices were told to mind, as they were so similar. (Another trade that claims the origin of this expression is the publican, the letters standing for 'pints and quarts' – writing out bills the two could easily be confused.) Printers are also said to have coined the phrase **the dog's bollocks**, it being their slang for the ':-' symbol.

Secondhand books

God's copy – a book in exceptionally good condition

squizz binding – an elaborate or beautiful one (short for 'exquisite')

hospital copy – a defective book, retained so that when other copies of the same title come along the various good parts can be pieced together

breaker – book whose illustrated plates have been removed for sale as prints. (Not a respectable practice.)

marriage – matching a jacketless book with a lone jacket of the same title

dog – an unsaleable book

inky – a book printed before 1500

I Sell By Numbers dealer – one who uploads his stock to eBay by swiping their barcodes to list the ISBN number. Seen as a soulless way of doing business.

Advertising

Some jargon from those cunning people whose messages take up so much (and pay for so much) of the media ...

above the fold – in web advertising, a message placed so that you don't need to scroll down to see it (comes from newspapers)

bleed – an ad that runs right to the edge of the page. One that doesn't (i.e. leaves a border) is **squared-up**. One that runs across both facing pages in a magazine is said to **bleed across the gutter**.

rewarded comprehension – aspect of an ad designed to make the customer feel pleased with himself for understanding it

reward shot – the one in a beer advert where a man takes a swig of the drink after a hard day's work

blue boat – deliberately useless component of an advert, inserted for picky clients so that they'll demand its removal and feel they've had their say. The rest of the ad can then be left as the agency intended. The term derives from Scotch whisky ads, where an ugly blue boat would be put in the middle of the loch.

trips to Disneyland – uncomfortable and miserable trips to the Scottish Highlands to present ads to distillery owners who would complain 'That disnae work. That disnae look good ...'

shelf-shout (US) – the aspects of a product's appearance that grab customers' attention

ENTERTAINMENT

THEATRE
FILM and TELEVISION
MUSIC BUSINESS
CIRCUSES and FUNFAIRS

THEATRE

ENTERTAINMENT

Just as entertaining as the plays and films we watch can be the terms that are bandied around backstage and off-screen by those involved in the production. Theatre actors talk about **tabs** (curtains), **angels** (the financial backers of a production) and **West End Wendies** (actors working in London's theatreland). In the movie business there's the **Martini shot** (the last one of the day), **deepies** (3D films) and **space operas** (sci-fi films). Meanwhile over in the world of music, sheet music is **dots**, a trombone is a **slush pump**, and roadies refer to **clown noses** (foam microphone covers). So why don't we settle into our seats, wait for the lights to dim, and enjoy some more entertainment jargon?

Theatre

Actors can be **DLP** (Dead Letter Perfect – absolutely on top of their lines), or can **phone it in** (give a performance so perfunctory that they might as well be doing it from home). On the night they might **go red/amber/green** (various stages of forgetting their lines, or **drying** – red is a total dry requiring prompt or help from fellow actor, green is OK). **Prompt** and **op** (opposite prompt) are used instead of 'stage right' and 'stage left' (the prompter used to sit in the wings), while the stage itself is the **green** (short for **greengage**).

dark (adj) – a theatre which hasn't got a show on

iron – metal safety-curtain

legit – serious drama, as opposed to musicals, comedy, and so on

leg-business – ballet-dancing

paper the house – give tickets away to fill the theatre and create an impression of a successful show

voms – the aisles (short for **vomitorium**)

The reason actors refer to Macbeth as **the Scottish play** is that in previous centuries the play was always seen as a sure-fire success, meaning that failing productions could be replaced by it at any minute. So if you saw actors rehearsing it (or even mentioning its name), you knew your current job was about to come to an end.

Break a leg, actors' traditional substitute for 'good luck', came about when Samuel Foote, manager of the Theatre Royal, Haymarket (then called the Little Theatre) boasted about his horsemanship. To bring him down a peg or two the Duke of York deliberately gave him a bad horse, which led to Foote breaking his leg (as it were). The Duke felt so guilty that he granted Foote a Royal warrant for the theatre. (Another group of people who think it unlucky to say the words 'good luck', incidentally, are the SAS.)

Quoth the raven – a phrase written by variety performers staying in digs. Expected to sign the visitor's book, they couldn't be uncomplimentary as this would risk unfavourable treatment by the landlady. So as a coded warning to other performers that their kind words weren't to be believed, they would add 'quoth the raven' at the end. This comes from Edgar Allen Poe's poem: 'Quoth the Raven: "Nevermore".'

The Glums – Les Miserables

Over in America, meanwhile, a **four-wall** is a theatrical contract where the producer assumes responsibility for all of the expenses of a show and gets all of the revenue, commonly used in Las Vegas. A contract where the theatre and the artist share expenses and revenue is a two-wall.

19th century British theatrical slang

A **rum cull** was the manager of a travelling theatre, in charge of **mummers** (the actors), or occasionally **barnstormers** (travelling players who performed in said buildings – hence the modern phrase). Another type of venue was the **penny gaff** (a shop temporarily turned into a theatre – enticing pictures of the performers would be displayed outside, alongside coloured lamps and so on). The stage manager was the **daddy**. To **mug up** was to apply your make-up and put on your costume. The orchestra was the **menagerie**, the curtain was the **jigger**, while **paradise** was the gallery (because you were 'up in the Gods'). **Clap-trap** was an ostentatious performance contrived simply to gain applause, perhaps indulged in by a **surf** (third-rate actor, frequently semi-professional).

The ghost doesn't walk meant you wouldn't be paid this week, as opposed to **the Mutton Walk**, which was the saloon at the Drury Lane theatre.

US vaudeville

The golden age of American vaudeville had many different types of performers. There was the **banana** (the comic, always ranked according to billing, hence the phrase **top banana**), the **peeler** (the stripper), the **roper** (the cowboy act) and the **Protean act** (the quick change act, Proteus being a Greek god who could change form). Those engaged in **chapeaugraphy** bent and twisted a large stiffened felt hat into different shapes to depict a variety of characters, while **chasers** were the performers at the end of the bill, so bad that they 'chased' audience stragglers out of the theatre. (Such performers would **play to the haircuts**, i.e. the back of the departing audience's heads.) An **in-one** was an act that only required the front six feet of the stage (i.e. in front of the first curtain); an **in-two** act required the next six feet, all the way up to a **full stage** act. A **mountaineer** was a performer who frequented the **Borscht Belt**, a string of resorts in the Catskill mountains catering mostly to Jewish audiences. Sometimes a double act would **lecture the skull** (the straight man talked,

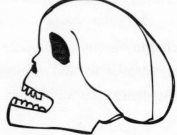

supposedly unaware that the comic was making faces behind him – from the 'skull' scene in Hamlet in which actors would mug behind Hamlet's back).

the beach – the area opposite a city's main theatre, where theatrical agencies were also to be found (in New York it was in Times Square, opposite the Palace Theatre) – so many performers looking for work would congregate in that area that they were seen as 'vacationing' there

blue material – the reason risqué or explicit material has come to be known as 'blue' dates from the days of E.F. Albee, a vaudeville boss noted for insisting that performers stick to clean material. If they transgressed they would receive a note from him, contained in a blue envelope, telling them which lines had to be cut from the act. They were better off sticking to a **Boston version** (a sanitised version of a routine – the Boston censors were notoriously strict).

claque – group of audience members paid to applaud a particular act, and possibly boo his competitors. (Applause itself was known as **mitting**.)

Gutenberg – a portable wardrobe containing your stage clothes (previously known as a **press**)

nut house – a theatre known for putting on comic acts

quarter – the '15 minutes to showtime' call

sleeper jump – the dressing room on the highest floor, reserved for those lowest on the bill. (So far away you had to take an overnight train to reach it.)

Toby time – white performers' slang for the TOBA circuit (Theatre Owners Booking Agency), which catered to black audiences but was owned by whites. Known by black performers as 'Tough on Black Asses'.

Bad acts (or **fish**, as in 'stinks like a ...') might **chew the scenery** (overact) or deliver **Joe Millers** (corny jokes – refers to the joke book authored by the performer of that name, who lived from 1684–1738 and is mentioned in *A Christmas Carol* by Charles Dickens: 'Joe Miller never made such a joke as sending [the turkey] to Bob's will be!') A **lard actor** was a performer who couldn't make enough money to buy cold cream with which to remove his make-up, having to use lard instead. (As lard was ham fat, this was also the derivation of **ham** for a bad actor.) If you were truly awful you might **get back your pictures** (be fired – your promotional photos from the lobby displays were returned to you) or even have to **take the veil** (retire from the stage, from the Catholic phrase for becoming a nun).

Film and television

We've all heard '**it's a wrap**' – but how many of us know that, instead of meaning 'wrap up' it actually stands  for 'wind reel and print'? Film and TV sets are a hotbed of slang, from the **teddy bear's arsehole** (the felt ring around the eyepiece of a viewfinder) to the **hobbit** (a small runner hiding somewhere in shot, ready to hold open a door or perform a similar task). You can **Spanish** something or someone (remove them from the shot – **Spanish archer** meaning elbow), or have a **ten-one** (a break to urinate, **ten-two** being a related term).

But just as Hollywood is the spiritual home of motion pictures, so the Americans have taken television and movie slang to new heights. There are **nabes** (local, i.e. neighbourhood cinemas), **moppets** (child actors) and **kudocasts** (awards shows). A film can be **helmed** (directed), then have its **bow** (premiere) and become a **click** (a hit). Sometimes this takes time: a **sleeper** is a movie or TV programme that achieves eventual success despite attracting little initial interest. You can **narrowcast** (air programming aimed at a specialist audience), possibly on **feevee** (pay-TV). This might be a **kidvid** (children's show) or a **zitcom** (a comedy aimed at teenagers). A **backdoor pilot** is a pilot episode deliberately made as a stand-alone film, so that it can be broadcast even if the whole series isn't commissioned, whereas a **busted pilot** is one that never gets broadcast.

ankle – a term that deliberately blurs the line between being fired and resigning, e.g. 'John Smith has ankled his position at Big Productions'

boff/boffo/boffola – outstanding (said of a film's performance at the box office) also **socko**, **whammo**, and **hotsy**

chopsocky – the martial arts genre

coin – financing for a film ('Coin for the project was raised by ...')

distribbery – a distribution company

dramedy – a comedy-drama

green light – approval for a movie to be made

horse opera – a Western (also known as an **oater**)

HUT – Homes Using Television ('HUT levels usually fall during the summer')

ink – to sign a contract

irritainment – an annoying but compulsive programme

the Lion – MGM (taken from the studio's famous logo). Similarly Disney is known as **the Mouse House**, and the ABC network as **the Alphabet Web**.

nix – to reject. This appeared in the headline of a famous story in *Variety*, Hollywood's trade paper, concerning rural audiences shunning films about life in the country: 'Sticks Nix Hick Pix'

nuts – expenses ('This Broadway show needs to operate at 60% of capacity to cover its nuts')

pour – a drinks party

ozoner – an open-air movie theatre (as opposed to an indoor one, which is a **hardtop**). Open-air theatres are also known as **passion pits**.

threequel – the sequel to a sequel

spotting a fin – detecting the first sign of a TV series going downhill – derives from **jumping the shark**, which is what a series is said to do when it starts 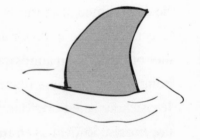 having to resort to a ludicrous plot devices. In a 1977 episode of *Happy Days*, the Fonz jumped over a shark while waterskiing.

sudser – a soap-opera

tentpole – a studio's biggest-grossing blockbuster of the season

unspool – to screen a film

wicket – the box office (the actual place, rather than the generic term for sales)

While actually shooting a film (or **lensing** it), a director will deal with his **talking props** (actors – also **meatpuppets**). He might have to **steal** (film on the street without getting the necessary permits). There'll be the **Abby Singer** – the second-last shot of the day (named after the assistant director Abner E. Singer, who used to pretend this was actually the last shot of the day). In a musical he'll deal with **cleffers** (songwriters), **terpers** (dancers – in Greek mythology Terpsichore ruled over dance) and **thrushes** (female singers, also known as **chantoosies**).

In the old days, if everything went wrong, there was always **Alan Smithee**, the fictitious director whose name appeared on the credits of any film from which the real director wanted to dissociate himself. The name was invented for the 1968 film *Death of a Gunfighter*. Neither of the two directors who'd worked on it wanted to receive a credit, so the Directors Guild of America decided to invent a name. At first they chose 'Al Smith', but then decided that was too common a name, so they lengthened the surname by two letters and turned 'Al' into 'Alan'. One critic liked the film, though confessed that the director was one 'I'm not familiar with'.

Over the years more and more directors took refuge behind the name – dozens of feature films and television episodes are credited to Alan Smithee. Then in 1998, the movie *An Alan Smithee Film: Burn Hollywood Burn* appeared, in which Eric Idle played a director unfortunate enough to have the name Alan Smithee, thereby rendering him unable to take his name off the credits of a film he wishes to distance himself from. Incredibly, the real-life director of *Burn Hollywood Burn* Arthur Hiller, protested about the producer interfering with his control, and so insisted on the name 'Alan Smithee' being used in the credits. *An Alan Smithee Film* became an Alan Smithee film. So notorious did this story become that the DGA formally retired the name. Alan Smithee, who had never existed, ceased to exist.

Other personnel involved in the industry include **percenters** (agents), **praisers** (publicists), and **Solons** (industry experts, from Solon, the Athenian statesman and poet)

Voiceover artists

Some terms from those people whose disembodied voices sell us washing powder or invite us to watch the latest BBC1 primetime drama ...

a Clarkson – the pause before the final word or words. 'The best shampoo [pause] your hair could wish for.'

on a green – start speaking when the green cue light flashes

cans – headphones. (Also **desperates** – short for **Desperate Dans**)

rock'n' roll – editing on the fly. Done sometimes with

narrations or audio books: when the voiceover artist makes a mistake the engineer rewinds, plays up until the error, then hits record and the artist seamlessly continues.

pop – a plosive 'p' sound (or other hard consonant) that **bends the needle** (distorts the recording)

chocolate – the use of graphic equalisation to make a voice rich and dark (very similar to **gravy browning**, meaning a rich delivery – known in the 1970s as a **brown ale voice**)

'Happy Christmas!' – said after an amusing mistake, knowing that the clip will be on the Christmas tape of outtakes that studios like to compile

shoulder-pad read – corporate-style delivery

'Can you hear my cleavage?' – asked by female voiceover artists to check if their delivery was sexy enough

voice of God – the unseen announcer at awards ceremonies and the like

The music business

Those who provide us with our tunes seem to have a fine ear for language too, though there seems to be a dividing line between the worlds of jazz and classical music, and that of pop. In the former it's the musicians themselves who originate slang, while in the latter the jargon comes from the roadies.

Jazz musicians can play the **bull-fiddle** (double bass, also known as a **dog-house**), a **liquorice stick** (clarinet), a **pretzel** (French horn, its player being a **pretzel-bender**) or a **woodpile** (xylophone). **Woodshedding**, on the other hand, is intensive private practice on your own. There's also **monkey-hurdler** for an organist.

In a classical orchestra you'll find **scrape, bang and blow** (the string, percussion and horn sections, the final one also sometimes known as the **kitchen**), while a **fixed chair** is a player with a title before their name (principal, assistant principal, and so on). In America the **carver** is the conductor ('Who's carving this gig?')

Orchestral scores contain rehearsal marks that have letter names. When announcing the conductor will often use the Cockney alphabet:

A for 'orses, B for mutton, C for yourself, etc

Frequently-performed composers with difficult-to-pronounce names quickly attract slang versions. Dmitri Shostakovich is **Shosty**, Sergei Rachmaninoff is **Rock**, and Sergei Prokofiev is **Proke**. The same principle applies to pieces of music. Rachmaninoff's *Rhapsody on a Theme of Paganini* is known as **Rock Pag**, while his Symphony No. 2 is **Rocky II**. Two one-act operas, *Cavalleria Rusticana* and *I Pagliacci*, are often performed on the same bill and are known as **Cav & Pag**.

American orchestras have the same tradition. Ravel's *Bolero* is **Bordello**, Schubert's 9th is **the Great C Monster**, while the *Bartered Bride Overture* is **the Battered Broad**. Poulenc's *Dialogue of the Carmelites* becomes **the Diarrhoea of the Caramels**, and Tchaikovksy's *Nutcracker Suite* the **Nutscratcher**.

Roadies

These doubty workers have jargon to describe lots of things, not least themselves. There are **lampies** (lighting technicians) and **vidiots** (members of a film crew), while a **neck down** is any member of the stage crew who doesn't have to think, merely carry out orders given by a more senior colleague. A **Wilkins** is a self-important employee of the venue, unconnected to the road crew themselves. Over in the United States, the lighting director is the **blinkie** (also **squint**), a **woodnymph** is a carpenter, and the **cotton tech** is the person selling the band's T-shirts. A **briefcase engineer**, on the other hand, is a roadie who never helps with the heavy stuff.

Then there's the equipment. A **P45 button** is any button on a mixing desk which if pressed would cause massive technical problems, thereby losing you your job. The **DFA** is a fake knob installed on the mixing desk which can be turned to full to pacify bands who want more treble/bass/etc (stands for 'does f*** all'). There are **gig spanners** (bottle-openers) and **gig**

turds (pieces of electrical tape that stick to your boot), while an **albatross** is any faulty piece of equipment for which the roadie who broke it has to remain responsible until it can be repaired. A **Kiwi road case** is a cardboard box, much as in America a **Mexican speed wrench** is a very big hammer. You can use an **LB** (a power adapter with one male and two female sockets – 'lucky bastard') or a **VLB** (a one-male-*three*-female adapter – 'very lucky bastard').

American roadies refer to the **resumé on a rope** (backstage passes from previous tours you've worked on worn round your neck – usually seen as bragging) and the **redneck laser** (mirrorball). There's also the **snake case** (a box that tidies all the different cables running from the stage) and the **toast rack** (stand that holds multiple guitars).

aquarium (US) – the area on the side of the stage where the guitars are kept, so-called because during the gig it fills up with hangers-on, meaning the guitar tech has to **swim** through them to get to the instruments

Belgium – to turn a case upside down so its wheels are pointing to the sky (a very black piece of humour, relating to the *Herald of Free Enterprise* ferry that capsized in 1987 shortly after leaving the Belgian port of Zeebrugge)

Betty (US) – a groupie

Billies – audience members ('Billy Bunters' – punters)

boner lounge (US) – the rear bunk in a tour bus

CHIPS (US) – 'Cleverly Hidden In Plain Sight' – reply to anyone looking for something that's right in front of him

crew chew (US) – roadies' food

doing the paperwork – rolling a joint

ego riser (US) – the short bit of stage that allows the lead singer to get closer to the crowd

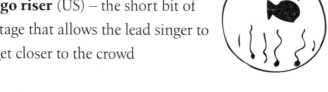

feed the fish (US) – throw used plectrums into the crowd at the end of the stage

germ (US) – a fan who met you once and now always pesters you for tickets

gig pig – an unattractive would-be groupie

GIGO (US)– Garbage In Garbage Out – response to a band complaining about a bad sound mix

HAMSTER (US) – Hooker Actress Model Stripper Trainer Entertainer Runaway – female who hangs around backstage hoping to 'meet' the band

'I'm not f***ing the monkey, I'm just holding his arms down' (US) – I'm not in charge, don't ask me

percussive maintenance – hitting something in an attempt to mend it

RAF – a Real Ale Fart

talent – the band (described by some roadies as a 'one-word oxymoron')

truck bongo – an erection caused by vibration while driving a lorry

Circuses and funfairs

The smell of the greasepaint, the roar of the crowd –
and an awful lot of slang. There are **giraffes** (very tall
unicycles), **barnburners** (performances so startling
they metaphorically set the place on fire) and **pigs**
(any animal with small eyes, even an elephant or a
bear). A very funny performance
is known in America as **aisles**
(the audience will be rolling
there), while a **straw house** is
a sold-out performance (straw
used to be spread on the ground
for extra spectators to sit on).
Other terms include:

antipodist (US) – a juggler who stands on his head
and juggles with his feet

bally (US) – a free performance given to attract people
to a nearby sideshow

buffer – a performing dog

bump a nose (US) – clowns' equivalent of 'break a leg'

dukkering – fortune telling

joey (US) – a clown (derived from Joseph Grimaldi, the famous 18th century English clown)

liberty horse (US) – one that performs without a rider

picture gallery (US) – a heavily-tattooed man

plush (US) – toy animals given away as prizes

rubber cow (US) – elephant

sponge plunge (US) – high dive into a frighteningly small amount of water

'Would John Robinson please come to the entrance' (US) – coded announcement telling current performer to cut their act short

Beware the games you play at funfairs. Many of them are **flats** (crooked ones at which the player can't win), such as the **Ikey Heyman** (a wheel of fortune to which the operator can surreptitiously apply a brake). In America, funfair workers (who call themselves **carnies**) might **burn the lot** (cheat customers with little attempt to conceal the cheating, done when they don't expect to visit the town again). They also refer to their **shill** (an accomplice who plays the game and wins in order to encourage other customers to come forward).

Meanwhile, the business and backstage element of the industry has its own terms. There is **jarry** (food, short for *mangiare*, Italian for 'to eat'), and (in the US) **patch money** (bribes paid to policemen to turn a blind eye) and **rat sheets** (advance posters making derogatory claims about competing circuses). Non-circus people are **flatties**, though the Americans know some of them as **lot lice** (the ones who stand around watching the circus being constructed, getting in the way).

and cakes (US, antiquated) – denoted that a performer would be provided with board as well as payment

dressing the house (US) – sell tickets in a pattern so that all sections have at least someone in, leaving no obviously empty areas (similar to, but subtly different from, **papering the house** in theatre slang)

fink (US) – broken (also **larry**)

grouch bags (small ones worn under the clothing to hold the performer's money and valuables, which might otherwise be stolen from the dressing room)

Mr and Mrs Wood and all the little Woods – empty seats at a show

peek his poke (US) – see how much money a possible customer has in his wallet

stake bites (US) – injuries to ankles sustained by walking into metal stakes while crossing the circus site in the dark

St Louis (US) – seconds of food (St Louis circus engagements were always played in two sections)

Windy Van Hooten's (US)– name of a mythical circus fondly imagined by performers, where pay, conditions and suchlike are all perfect

First of May (US) – a novice performer or worker (that being the traditional opening date for circuses). Another term for the same thing is a **forty miler**, the implication being that they're someone who has never been more than that distance from home.

jump (US) – the period of time when the carnies take down the funfair and move to another location

THE MILITARY

THE MILITARY

Life in the military, it seems, is a veritable assault course of jargon. You don't have medals in the Army, you have **brag rags**. A telling-off is an **interview without coffee**. The Navy has its **sun dodgers** (submariners) and **louse ladders** (sideburns), while instead of going to bed, members of the RAF **climb up and level at two foot six**. They also, with a rather darker sense of humour, refer to a nuclear weapon as a **bucket of sunshine**. So strap on your **battle bowler** (First World War slang for a steel helmet) there's plenty of incoming slang to deal with here ...

The Army

Had your **rag fair** (kit inspection)? Engaged in some **bags of smoke and straight up the middle** (taken the direct and obvious approach)? Then you're in the British Army. This is the institution where **on the carpet** means at ground level and **ack emma** means in the morning (from the old signalling terms for the letters A and M, **pip emma** being the afternoon). The Army don't use Morse Code any more – but when they did it was **iddy-umpty**.

Soldiers are sometimes known as **lobsters** (because they used to wear red coats), while a **brain on a chain** is a dog handler. The chaplain is the **sky pilot**, while a sergeant is **stripey**. (In the US Army a full colonel is a **chicken colonel**, the badge of that rank being an eagle.) **Woodentops** are the Guards, named after their bearskin headdress, which used to be wood-lined. Meanwhile a **green** is a particularly keen soldier (such personnel are also said to **bleed green**). In the Navy anyone displaying enthusiasm is **anchor-faced**. (Incidentally 'green' is also bookmakers' slang for an inexperienced horse.)

the Andrew – Army nickname for the Royal Navy. (Pressgang leader Andrew Miller was said to have owned the Royal Navy.)

beasting – running someone into the ground

bowler hat – to discharge someone (the **golden bowler** being a discharge followed by a job at the Ministry of Defence)

chinstrapped – very tired – (as in being so tired that the only thing stopping you from falling down is the strap on your headgear)

click – a kilometre

coffeepot – nuclear reactor

(to be put on a) fizzer – to be officially charged with doing something wrong

Hollywood shower – an excessively long shower (meanwhile in the RAF an 'Army shower' is applying deodorant instead of washing)

noduf – term used on an exercise to denote that you really do have a casualty, this isn't part of the exercise

phys – any form of exercise

scratcher – sleeping bag (also **doss bag**)

'skin is waterproof' – a standard line when complaining about having no waterproofs

threaders – tired or bored

'You've only been in since Naafi break' – said to a soldier with little experience

When you're actually engaged in action, you might **get around the bazaars** (survey the situation) or resort to a **shovel recce** (defecating in a field). **Hard target** means to run from cover to cover, while a **Roman candle** is a landing where your parachute fails to open. **'Wait out'** said on the radio means 'I'll get back to you', while **'say again'** is a request to do just that; soldiers never use the word **'repeat'** as this is a request to the artillery to send more shells your way. British soldiers fighting in Afghanistan in the 21st century refer to the consequence of stepping on a landmine as **pink mist**.

Blighty, meaning home, derived from the Hindustani word *vilayati* (pronounced 'bilati' in many Indian dialects) meaning a foreigner. Another Indian word that found its way into Army slang is **dhobi**, the caste of people who wash clothes. To this day you **dhobi** your clothes using **dhobi dust** (washing powder).

First World War slang

The Army's jargon has changed down the years. Back in World War I, **hate** meant bombardment from the Germans, while severe bombardment was **Jericho**. **Gooseberry** was barbed wire, the steel post for staking it in the ground being a **corkscrew** (after the shape at its end enabling it to be twisted quietly into the ground – previously, the noise of hammering stakes in had attracted enemy fire).

An **egg** was a hand grenade, and a **hipe** a rifle (from drill sergeants' habit of giving the last word of an order a crisper delivery, so that 'slope arms!' became 'slope hipe!'). The Lewis light machine gun was the **Belgian rattlesnake**.

Away from the front line, **canteen medals** were beer or food stains on the breast of a tunic, and **gunfire** was strong tea, often laced with rum

become a landowner – to be buried

before your number was dry – expression used by more experienced soldiers to new recruits. 'I was killing Germans before your number was dry' (in ink on the enlistment form).

billjim – an Australian (two popular Australian names of the time)

a Blighty one – a wound serious enough to require the recipient to be sent home. (The Americans had a comparable term during Vietnam: the USA was known as 'the world', and a Blighty one was known to US soldiers as a **ticket to the world**.)

canary – instructor (they wore yellow armbands)

cold meat ticket – identity disc. Men were issued with discs giving their name, number, unit and religion. The disc remained with the body after death.

the Forty-Tens – 2nd Battalion, The Leinster Regiment. Derived from one of their members who, being the fiftieth man on parade and having just heard 'forty-nine', called out 'forty-ten'.

hom forty – French railway carriage used for troop transportation. From the capacity stencilled on the side of the carriage: 'Hommes 40, Chevaux 8'.

third man – to go too far. A popular superstition on the Western Front was that the third man to light his cigarette from the same match would be killed. Enemy snipers would, at night, use the flame of the match to find a target – the first light alerted the sniper, the second allowed him to aim, and the third time he fired.

Second World War US Army slang

Uncle Sam's finest have always been ready with the jargon, not least during World War II. A **Chicago atomizer** was an automatic rifle, and an **iron horse** a tank. The latter could be driven in **Grandma** (low gear) or **Rachel** (high gear). A shovel was an **Army banjo**, and a **brolly** was a parachute. If you dropped a bomb you **laid an egg** or **left a calling card**. As with British soldiers in World War I, there were also non-combat terms. Many related to food: **army strawberries** were prunes, **Irish grapes** were potatoes and **Lot's wife** was salt. To wash it down you might have **battery acid with sidearms** (coffee with cream and sugar – not to be confused with a **sugar report**, which was a letter from your girlfriend). At the end of mealtimes it was over to the **pot walloper** (the washer-up).

Royal Air Force

In the RAF new technology is **Gucci**, **dangling the Dunlops** is lowering your undercarriage, and a **hydraulic palm tree** is a helicopter. You can **get the coals on** (increase speed rapidly), **letterbox** (fly between low cloud and the ground) or, more prosaically, **build a shed** (get very drunk). **Auntie Betty** is the current Queen, though **Bitching Betty** is the recorded female voice in software that tells a pilot how to avoid collision. **Adolf Hitler**, in contrast, is a cup of tea that's white with one lump.

Down on **cumulo-granitus** (the ground) is the **handbrake house** (station HQ), where you may have a **mahogany bomber** (desk). After some **babbage** (a kebab) you might have to announce **'Badger!'** (a warning to colleagues that you have just broken wind). To **beak** is to talk loudly, while if you **show someone the hairy side** you are aggressive towards them (the hairy side being the back of your hand). Back at home is your **long-haired air marshal** (wife). If you're **beyond 10 West** you're far enough from home to permit infidelity to her.

Personnel include **seat-to-stick interfaces** (pilots –
highly-skilled ones are **stick ninjas**), **wops** (wireless
operators) and **meat bombs** (paratroopers). A **Jonny
two shits** is someone who brags about always
going one better; they're often said to **holiday in
Elevenerife**. In the old days a
penguin was a member of the
Women's RAF (a 'flapper who
didn't fly').

beano brief – list of prohibited
actions or places ('be' and 'no')

Bloggs – to perform a deliberate mistake when flying
to test the vigilance of your crew

bold underlined – very important

cummerbunds and waistcoats – alternative to the
phrase 'swings and roundabouts'

file bravo one November – throw away

mandraulically – performing by hand a task that's usually automated

motion lotion – fuel

o-dark hundred hours – very early in the morning

pain et beurre – the basics of something

sausage-side – in enemy territory

Scooby – a clue (short for **Scooby Doo**)

Smartie board – a map showing dots in various colours

takeoffs equal landings – said of someone who has never had to eject

zebra's arsehole – deep meteorological depression, shown on a chart as concentric and closely-spaced circles

Equipment includes **beeps and squeaks** (the electronics) and the **pickle button** (the one that fires a weapon). Sitting in the **greenhouse** (cockpit) you'll be wearing a **bonedome** (crash helmet) and praying you don't have to **exit via the sunroof** (use your ejector seat, or **bang seat**). **Ginners** is excellent visibility (from **gin clear**), which is what you want if you engage in an **octaflugeron** (complicated flying manoeuvre). This may be a **knife fight in a phone box** (close-quarters dogfight between two highly manoeuvrable planes), a

Mexican hat (flying in circles around the same location) or

thrupney bitting (turning through less than ninety degrees, repeating this so as to fly in the shape of a polygon around a fixed centre point). In an emergency you'll have to **kick the tyres and light the fires** (take off without your usual safety checks).

As that last phrase shows, some of the service's slang reflects the fact that life isn't always easy or straightforward. A **cake and arse party** is a pointless exercise, also known as **punching holes in the sky**; add an element of difficulty and it's **like pushing spaghetti up a wild cat's arse**. Someone who is **stuck on transmit** is garrulous. Sarcasm plays its part in RAF life. You might ask someone to **give you some granularity** (an ironic way of saying 'give me more details') or observe that the **pigs are fuelled and ready** (when someone predicts something you don't think will happen). Equally if you're perspiring a lot you are **sweating like an armourer in a spelling test**. **Spears on the outside**, meanwhile, is an order that there is to be no in-fighting among the group.

The RAF, as you might expect with a name like theirs, do love an acronym:

ALF/RALF – Annoying Little F***er/Really Annoying ...
BIC – said before something that is not to be repeated (short for 'Boys In Confidence')
FAUTMOB – F*** All Use To Man Or Beast
BOTOT – Bombs On Target On Time
POETS – P*** Off Early, Tomorrow's Saturday
SHAG – a junior team-member (short for 'Student Has A Go')

Royal Navy

Ever found yourself on a
bird farm (aircraft carrier)
in the middle of the **oggin**
(the sea)? If you know what this means then you're
probably a member of the Royal Navy. You might
be an **anchor clanker** (an ordinary seaman, also
known as a **deck ape**), a **bubblehead** (a scuba
diver), a **clankie** (a mechanical engineer) or even a
four-ringer (a captain). A **deeps** is a submariner,
while those who remain on the surface are **dabtoes**.
Navy pilots are **airdales**, electricians **amp tramps**,
and radio operators **bunts** (from the days when
messages were sent with semaphore flags, or **bunting**).
Personnel from the Fleet Air Arm personnel are
known as **Airy Fairies**,
while the Red Arrows are
the **Crimson Crabfats**.

Father Famine is the supply officer responsible for
food. He might conjure up **straight rush** (roast meat
and vegetables), **BITS** (beans in tomato sauce) or
tram smash (bacon and tinned tomatoes). **Thickers**
is condensed milk. Break a tooth while eating and

you'll have to see the **fang farrier** (dentist, also
known as the **molar mangler**).

amateur night – the day after
payday

baby spanner – penis (the male
genitalia in their entirety being
toggle and two)

barrack stanchion – sailor who avoids spells at sea

banyan – barbecue or party on the flight deck,
usually with steaks and beer. The term is derived from
banian, a garment worn by an East Indian sect which
neither kills nor eats meat (a banyan is a species of
tree). In the 18th century, the British Navy denied its
sailors meat on Mondays, Wednesdays, and Fridays;
these days were known as **banian days**. The term has
now come to mean just the opposite.

bunch of bastards – tangled-up ropes

Captain's table – disciplinary hearing

Dagenham Dave – someone who's one stop short of Barking (also known as **Harpic**, i.e. 'clean round the bend')

dung hampers – underpants

free gangway – permission to go ashore without formal inspection

Goat Locker – the chiefs' quarters and mess. The term originated during the era of wooden ships, when chiefs were given charge of the milk goats on board. Also known as the **Menopause Manor**.

hanging garden – hammocks suspended from the ceiling

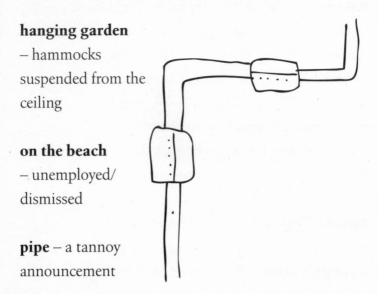

on the beach – unemployed/ dismissed

pipe – a tannoy announcement

proctoheliosis – condition whereby you believe the sun shines from your backside

putting the Queen to bed – lower the White Ensign at sunset

tin fish – a torpedo

two's up – reserve for next use (e.g. 'two's up with that book')

POLITICS

POLITICS

Chicago, we should remember, got its nickname of the **Windy City** not from its weather but because its politicians talked so much. Similarly on this side of the Atlantic, Neil Kinnock became known as the **Welsh Windbag**. When a profession talks as long and as hard as this one, slang will never be far away ...

Political players

Whether it's the British Chief Secretary to the Treasury (whose main job is to refuse spending requests from government departments) being known as the **Abominable No Man** or the President of the United States being the **POTUS** (and his wife, the First Lady, the **FLOTUS**), the people who play out political dramas rejoice in various nicknames. A **carpetbagger** is a representative with no historical connections to his constituency (in 19th century America the carpet bag was a popular means of carrying your possessions), while a **snollygoster** is someone who wants to be elected simply for the sake of it, not caring about principles or policies (possibly derived from the German *schnelle geister* – quick spirit). An **actorvist** is a celebrity who gets involved in politics, at the opposite end of the energy scale from **slacktivism** (activism that requires little effort).

The early 1970s saw **chocolate soldiers** in the British Parliament; they were assistants to Opposition spokesmen whose salaries were funded by the Joseph Rowntree Social Service Trust. Not to be confused with a **self-licking lollipop**, an institution that exists primarily to ensure its own survival. Other food-inspired names include **room meat** (the ordinary people who stand or sit on the platform behind politicans at conference speeches and campaign announcements), **watermelon** (an environmentalist who used to be a socialist – green on the outside, red on the inside), and **cookie-pusher** (an American official who does little but attend tea parties). Also over the pond, a **theoconservative** is a member of the religious right, while a **Paleoconservative** is a holder of old-fashioned or extreme right-wing beliefs. Someone supporting policies seen as harmful to the environment is a **pollutitian**.

Whipping (getting your own side to vote as they should) is crucial. Westminster has been known to use **toilet whips** (those assigned to sitting in cubicles to eavesdrop on conversations of male MPs using the urinals), and American parties employ **visibility whips** to ensure that placards are seen at political conventions.

Particular individuals attract their own nicknames. The Labour minister Geoff Hoon became known as **Buff** Hoon, while Tory MP David Ruffley has been called **Treat Me**. Conservative politician Chris Patten called Margaret Thatcher by her middle name **Hilda** (though never to her face), and during Iain Duncan Smith's troubled time as Tory leader he was referred to as **In Deep Strife**. The bitterness between Tony Blair and Gordon Brown known as the **TeeBee GeeBees** led to the latter being dubbed the **Prime Mentalist**. The US military leadership under Secretary of Defense Donald Rumsfeld rejoiced in the unofficial title of **Rummy's Dummies**.

A political lexicon

Some more terms you'll need to get used to if you choose a political career ...

black swan moment – something that couldn't possibly have been predicted

catastrof*** – a serious political disaster (if it gets even worse it becomes an **Af*******alypse Now**)

Dover test – the level of casualties the American public is prepared to accept in a war (Dover Air Force Base in Delaware is where US soldiers' bodies are flown back to)

Eurocreep – the gradual acceptance of the Euro during its early years in countries which hadn't officially adopted it

lights-on bill (US) – a measure introduced so that a public body is funded at only the most basic level

off the reservation (US) – out of step with your party's official position

physics package – euphemism used by politicians for a nuclear warhead

prayers – British ministerial meetings at 9.30 each morning

schoolgate issue – a day-to-day topic discussed by mothers collecting their children from school (known in Australia as a **barbecue stopper**)

Super-Duper Tuesday – a Super Tuesday (important day for US Presidential primary elections) on which more elections than usual are held

Trashcanistan (US) – any poor Middle Eastern country/central Asian republic

the waterfront – the **bigger-picture** policies across all government departments – one adviser will be paid to **see the waterfront**

Acronyms

Politicians do like a good set of initials ...

BANANA – someone opposed to any new building projects (Build Absolutely Nothing Anywhere Near Anyone)

BOGSAT – decision-making by a small collection of associates (Bunch Of Guys Sat Around a Table)

CGSM – unimportant information (Consignment of Geriatric Shoe Makers – i.e. a load of old cobblers)

FLOHPA – mythical state deemed to be important in the 2004 US Presidential election (Florida, Ohio and Pennsylvania were seen as crucial battlegrounds)

PUSSY – Parliamentary Under-Secretary of State – the lowest ministerial rank in the British government

Senior civil servants are traditionally made a Companion of the Order of St Michael and St George (the CMG), a Knight Commander of the same order (KCMG), or a Knight Grand Cross (GCMG). In the service these are said to stand for **Call Me God**, **Kindly Call Me God** and **God Calls Me God.**

American government bodies known by their initials are sometimes called **alphabet agencies**

Groupings

Political success is all about getting people behind you. This might be achieved by a **big tent** approach (allowing a wide range of views among the members of your party), or relying on an **amen corner** (a group of supporters who give you their unconditional support). An **echo chamber** is a group of people who constantly reinforce each other's ideas, while a group of individuals or organisations with complicated and overlapping connections to each other are a **spaghetti bowl**. Beware an **Astro-Turf** – it's a supposedly spontaneous grass-roots movement that has actually been organised from above.

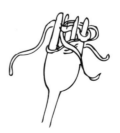

Sometimes groupings are along the lines of race. **Amexica** is the area either side of the US/Mexico border that shares a common culture and language, and **Hispandering** is the tendency to pay special attention to the concerns of the Hispanic community. The racial divide between the Deep South and the rest of the United States was sometimes known (after Europe's 'Iron Curtain') as the **Cotton Curtain**.

Fighting within parties is often more hostile than that between parties. Liberal Tories refer to the right-wing Cornerstone Group as the **Tombstone Group**, and Norfolk traditionalists who opposed the Conservative leadership's modernising policies were christened the **Turnip Taliban**. Eurosceptics sometimes refer to Europhiles as **federasts**. The European nations (such as France and Germany) who opposed early 21ˢᵗ century US foreign policy became known in America as the **Axis of Weasel**.

While we're talking insults, the Scottish Parliament at Holyrood has been called the **Numptorium**, and those who downplay the threat of international terrorism have been accused of having a **September 10th viewpoint**. Political correctness carried to ludicrous levels is sometimes known as **bollitics**. The term **bunkum**, meaning 'rubbish', derives from a lengthy 1820 speech by state representative Felix Walker, of Buncombe County, North Carolina. Colleagues begged him to stop, because no one was listening. 'Never mind,' came Walker's reply, 'I'm talking to Buncombe.'

All this talk, though, is sometimes just that – talk. In which case it's **gorilla dust**, intimidatory language with no real intent. Gorillas toss clouds of dirt into the air when they confront each other, but rarely progress to actual fighting.

Tactics

Politics can be a tough old game, and you have to know what you're doing. There are **dog-whistle policies** (those, for instance on immigration, carefully phrased so as to mean one thing to your supporters while going unnoticed by everyone else) and **prebuttals** (answers to criticisms before they are made). You can **kick the can down the road** (avoid an awkward decision by postponing it) or **ratf***** (infiltrate an opposition group to undermine it – a term invented by Richard Nixon's aide Donald Segretti). There's **blinkmanship** (a no-concessions bargaining technique), **push polling** (spreading damaging information about your opponent under the guise of conducting an independent telephone survey) and the **shit sheet** (a campaign document rubbishing a rival party).

decapitation tactic – targeting vulnerable marginal constituencies held by the opposing party in a general election

doughnut tactic – Boris Johnson's strategy for winning the London Mayoralty in 2008 (he concentrated on the city's outer constituencies, knowing he had little chance in the inner city ones). Not to be confused with **doughnutting**, which is the practice of seating women on the House of Commons benches to the side of and behind the Prime Minister to create a friendly impression of the party to television viewers.

earbuying – lobbying

faggot vote (19th century) – practice of splitting residential property into separate flats to allow more people at the address to vote

fill the tree (US) – proposing amendments to your own Senate bill to stop anyone else doing so (a Senate bill can have only a limited number of amendments – a 'tree')

game – think through possible implications of an announcement (predicting what your opponents will say, how you'll respond to them and so on, as in the phrase '**Have you gamed this?**')

granny farming – putting pressure on supporters in old people's homes to vote, possibly by organising minibuses to take them to the polling station

just-in-time politics – making up policy in response to the news rather than long-held beliefs

late train – support for a candidate offered after his election victory

neverendum – series of referenda held until the establishment's desired result is achieved

packing and cracking – redrawing constituency boundaries for party political purposes – the former is pulling more of your supporters into an area, the latter splitting an opposing party's supporters into two constituencies

playing dead – a governing party tacitly encouraging people to think it's a foregone conclusion that the opposition will win (in the hope that that party's supporters will then not bother to vote)

retail politics – campaigning centred around door-to-door canvassing. Concentrating on national media adverts is **wholesale politics**.

snooker clause (US) – one inserted into a bill very late on in its passage into law so as to avoid public attention

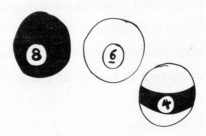

The Media

Nowadays much of the agenda is dictated by the **commentariat**, the body of radio and TV presenters and newspaper columnists who write about and debate politics, often engaging in **behindology** (studying the 'real' story behind politicians' spin). So elected representatives have to play the meejah game, be it by providing journalists with a **tick-tock** (a minute-by-minute account of a big event) or arranging a **spray** (a brief public meet-and-greet between two leaders at which they answer one or two questions but don't give a full press conference). At the latter you have to beware of **velcroids** – people who stand close to leaders to get public exposure. If you're flying overseas you can expect enquiries from journalists about the exact time of **wheels up/down** (when your plane takes off/lands).

On radio programmes such as **WATO** (pr. 'whatto', BBC Radio 4's politically-influential *The World At One*) you might take part in a **disco**, a discussion between the presenter and two guests (the presenter plus three guests being a **trisco**). After a leaders' debate during a general election the journalists head for **Spin Alley**, the room where party representatives try to convince them that their leader won. Mention might be made of the **worm**, a live opinion poll showing people's reactions as the debate progresses – the line goes up and down depending on whether people approve or disapprove of what is being said.

Out at lunch with a journalist he or she might do a **toilet job** (rushing to the loo to note down a story you've just given them). In America political types often engage in a **Washington read** (searching a book's index for mentions of their own name).

Cosy up to the media too much, though, and you could annoy your own supporters. When Tony Blair developed a habit of preferring easy TV chat-show appearances to serious news interviews, his MPs accused him of **democratic sofalism**.

FOOD AND DRINK

FOOD AND DRINK

Jargon, it would seem, is food
and drink to those who supply us
with our food and drink. When
a catering firm delivers food to a
client, leaving them to cook and
prepare it, they call it a **hump
and dump**. Brewers, meanwhile,
refer to water as **liquor**, and to the
haze of impurities that can form
at the bottom of a cask as **fluffy
bottoms**. Beer that's **sunstruck**

has been ruined by exposure to strong sunlight (it can

happen in seconds if you're drinking
outside; this is why beer bottles were
traditionally brown – clear or green
glass let the wrong wavelengths of
light through).

But it's in restaurants that the slang really gets
sizzling ...

Modern restaurants

From the **door whore** (hostess) through the **sponge monkey** (pastry chef) to the **cabbage mechanic** (low-ranking chef), every member of staff in a restaurant has their own lingo. Chefs refer to **Aldershot stock** (water) and **Scouse roux** (water and flour, used as a thickening agent). If they're **boxed off** they have all their preparation done, ready for service; the opposite is being **in the weeds** (in trouble, also known as **in the pommes frit**). They might use a **flabby dongler** (spatula), or execute a **BTF** (a steak order requesting 'very well done', i.e. 'burnt to f***'). **Ping cuisine** is microwaved food, achieved by applying some **radar love** in the **Bat Cave**. A **fanny** of something is a small amount of it.

Really basic tasks are carried out by the **kitchen bitch** (porter). The washing-up is done by the **dish pig**, though one London chef likes to call them **underwater ceramic engineers**, and they're also known as **skip**

rats because they're the first to eat any leftovers after service. In America they're known as **pearl divers** or **bubble dancers**.

While we're in the USA, **campers** are customers who linger all night, and a **chew and screw** is a diner who leaves without paying the bill. '**Corner!**' is a warning called out when you're approaching the same, to prevent collisions. To **peet** is to drink (from *A Clockwork Orange*) – this might be done from a **Freddy** (a bottle of Heineken beer, that being the Christian name of the brewery's founder) or a **weeper** (wine bottle with a leaky cork). When a beer bottle is empty it becomes a **dead soldier**. In Utah there is a piece of legislation known as the **chug law**: it forbids drinkers from having more than one drink in front of them, but has the opposite effect of that intended – when the waitress brings your second drink you end up 'chugging' the remains of the first.

American restaurants with scantily-clad female staff (for instance Hooters) are known as **breastrants**.

Pre WW2 American diners

The real heyday of restaurant slang was in America during the middle of the 20th century, when diners rechristened virtually their entire menus. This was often because they were such noisy places, and it was easy to mishear orders. For instance 'rye bread' could sound like 'white bread' – so it became **whisky** instead.

Eggs were **cackle berries** or **hen fruit**, and could be **deadeye** (poached), **wrecked** (scrambled) or  **blindfolded** (basted with their yolks unbroken). **Fry two and let the sun shine** meant two eggs with unbroken yolks, **cluck and grunt** was eggs and bacon, **two dots and a dash** was two fried eggs and a slice of bacon and **Adam and Eve on a raft** was two eggs on toast. **Eve with a lid**, on the other hand, was apple pie (Eve tempted Adam with an apple). **Eve with a mouldy lid** was apple pie with cheese. Staying with the Biblical couple, spare ribs were **first lady** (because Eve was made from that part of Adam's body).

Toast was **shingle** or **down** (from the act of lowering the bread into the toaster). **Brown down** was wheat toast. Other variations included:

dough well done with cow to cover – buttered toast

shingle with a shimmy and a shake – toast with butter and jam

mama on a raft – marmalade on toast

Pancakes were a **stack** or **a blowout patch** (because they resembled the pieces of rubber used to repair punctures on inner tubes). The syrup poured over them was **motor oil**. Butter was **cow paste**, **axle grease** or **skid grease**, and margarine was **smear**.

Also on the menu (without appearing on the menu) were:

Cow juice, **moo juice** or **baby juice** – milk (evaporated milk being **cow in a can**)

frog sticks – French fries (also known as **Joan of Arc**)

heart attack on a rack – biscuits and gravy (a dish comprising dough biscuits covered in a gravy made from dripping, flour and milk)

Irish turkey – corned beef and cabbage

life preserver – doughnut

Murphy – potatoes

Zeppelins – sausages (**Zeppelins in a fog** being sausages and mashed potato)

bullets – baked beans

breath – an onion

Italian perfume – garlic (also **Bronx vanilla**)

radio – tuna sandwich (possibly because 'tuna' sounds like 'tune')

one from the Alps – Swiss cheese sandwich. Grilled American cheese, on the other hand, was known as GAC and hence **Jack**. With bacon it was **Jack Benny**.

For breakfast you might have **birdseed** (cereal) or **sinkers and suds** (coffee and doughnuts).

Meatloaf was **butcher's revenge**, while beef stew was **bossy in a bowl**. Similarly **hash** was a dish made up of varying ingredients (some sort of meat, onions, potatoes, spices – the combination varied widely). So when this was ordered the waiter would instruct the cook to **sweep the kitchen floor**, or **customer will take a chance**. Hash on the side was **mystery in the alley**.

Instructions to the chef

You could **Pittsburgh** something (toast or char it, the city being known for its coal and steel production) or **burn the British** (toast an English muffin). **High and dry** was a sandwich without butter or dressing, **make it cry** was a dish with onions and **Mickey Rooney** meant add mustard and relish. A burger with lettuce and tomatoes would be **burn one, take it through the garden and pin a rose on it**. If you wanted it without lettuce the waiter would call **keep off the grass**. A rare steak was **still mooing**, **on the hoof** or **with the horns still on**, while a well-done steak was a **hockey puck**.

When it came to drinks, if orange juice was ordered, the waiter would shout **squeeze one** or **hug one**. Coffee was a **cup of mud**, **dirty water**, **Java**, **Joe** – or the waiter would just call **draw one**. Coffee variants included **blonde** (with cream), **blonde with sand** (with cream and sugar), **50/50 Joe** (with half-and-half), **in the dark** (black),

cowboy coffee (made with chicory), **Frosty Joe** (iced) and **Joe O'Malley** (Irish coffee).

Want tea instead? That was **boiled leaves**, or, if you wanted lemon, **a spot with a twist**. **Black cow** was chocolate milkshake, **white cow** vanilla milkshake and **hot top** a hot chocolate. **Balloon juice** was soda water, **city juice** was still water, while **belch water** was Alka Seltzer. **Atlanta** was Coca-Cola (home to the firm's headquarters), and **drag one through Georgia** meant add chocolate syrup to a Coke. Ice, meanwhile, was **hail**.

Other slang included:

biscuit-shooter – a waiter/waitress (also **hash-slinger** or **soup jockey**)

(a) crowd – three of something (four of something was a **bridge party**)

eighty-six – to remove an item from the menu, when it had run out. This is said to have originated in Chumley's, a legendary New York speakeasy during Prohibition, which had entrances on two intersecting streets, Bedford and Barrow. If the police raided the Barrow entrance, patrons would run out of the Bedford one, which was at number 86.

haemorrhage – ketchup

Ike and Mike – salt and pepper pots on the table (also **the twins**). Salt itself was **sea dust**.

lumber – a toothpick

on a rail or **on the fly** – in a hurry

PITA – a difficult customer (short for **pain in the ass**)

take it for a walk – a takeaway order (also **on wheels**)

yellow mud – mustard